101

Bestselling Success Book Summaries: Quotes and Lessons

Masresha Tekletsadik Gebre

DEDICATION

To all those who have ever dreamed of achieving success,
This book is for you. May the insights and wisdom contained
Within its pages inspire you to pursue your goals with
Passion, determination, and a relentless desire to learn and
Grow. Special thanks to Masresha Tekletsadik for his
Collaboration in bringing this project to life, and to open
Artificial Intelligence for its cutting-edge technology that
Made it all possible.

Content

ACKNOWLEDGMENTS

I would like to express my deepest gratitude to my beloved wife, Bezawit Chanyalew, whose unwavering support and encouragement have been invaluable throughout the writing of this book. Your love and dedication have been the driving force behind my work, and I couldn't have done it without you.

I also extend my thanks to open Artificial Intelligence, whose cutting-edge technology has made it possible to extract and analyze vast amounts of information from the best-selling books on success. Without AI's advanced machine learning algorithms, this book would not have been possible.

Finally, I would like to acknowledge the hard work and dedication of my book editor, who tirelessly worked to refine and polish the manuscript to its final form. Your keen eyes for detail and commitment to excellence have made a significant impact on the quality of this book.

Thank you all for your contributions, support, and commitment to this project. I am grateful beyond words.

INTRODUCTION

Success is a concept that has captivated humans for centuries. From the ancient Greeks to modern-day entrepreneurs, everyone seeks to achieve success in their personal and professional lives. However, with so much information available on the topic, it can be overwhelming to know where to start. That's where "101 Bestselling Success Book Summaries: Quotes and Lessons" comes in.

This groundbreaking book, Authored by Masresha Tekletsadik and open Artificial Intelligence, provides readers with a comprehensive overview of some of the most popular and influential books on the subject of success. Using state-of-the-art machine learning algorithms, AI has combed through a vast library of literary works to extract the most essential quotes, lessons, and summaries from each book.

The result is a concise, yet powerful compilation of insights that can help readers achieve their personal and professional goals. From Napoleon Hill's "Think and Grow Rich" to Stephen Covey's "The 7 Habits of Highly Effective People," this book provides readers with a one-stop-shop for all the information they need to succeed.

Whether you're an aspiring entrepreneur, a seasoned business executive, or simply someone who wants to achieve more in life, "101 Bestselling Success Book Summaries: Quotes and Lessons" is the ultimate guidebook for success. So, join us on this journey of discovery as we explore the wisdom and insights of some of the most successful minds in history.

CHAPTER 1

Personal Development and Growth

1. Think and Grow Rich by Napoleon Hill

Quotes

"Whatever the mind can conceive and believe, it can achieve."

"Strength and growth come only through continuous effort and struggle."

"Desire is the starting point of all achievement, not a hope, not a wish, but a keen pulsating desire which transcends everything."

"The starting point of all achievement is desire. Keep this constantly in mind. Weak desire brings weak results, just as a small fire makes a small amount of heat."

"Success requires no apologies, failure permits no alibis."

"There is one quality which one must possess to win, and that is definiteness of purpose, the knowledge of what one wants, and a burning desire to possess it."

"Education comes from within; you get it by struggle and effort and thought."

"The way of success is the way of continuous pursuit of knowledge."

"Every adversity, every failure, every heartache carries with it the seed of an equal or greater benefit."

"If you cannot do great things, do small things in a great way."

Lessons

"Think and Grow Rich" by Napoleon Hill is a classic self-help book that contains many valuable lessons for readers looking to achieve success and prosperity. Here are some of the key lessons that can be learned from this book:

The power of positive thinking: Hill emphasizes the importance of having a positive mental attitude, and suggests that focusing on one's goals and visualizing success can help bring it into reality.

The importance of persistence: Hill notes that successful people are often those who are willing to keep working toward their goals, even in the face of setbacks or failures.

The value of self-discipline: Hill suggests that successful people are often those who are able to control their impulses and stay focused on their goals, even when it's difficult.

The importance of taking action: Hill notes that it's not enough to simply think about success - one must also take action in order to make it a reality.

The value of networking: Hill suggests that building relationships and working with others can be a key component of achieving success.

The importance of continued learning: Hill notes that successful people are often those who are constantly learning and seeking to improve themselves and their knowledge.

The need for a definite purpose: Hill suggests that having a clear and specific goal is important for achieving success, and that one should focus on this purpose above all else.

The importance of faith: Hill suggests that having faith in oneself and one's ability to achieve success is essential for actually making it happen.

Overall, "Think and Grow Rich" offer readers a range of valuable lessons and insights for achieving success in life and business.

Summary

"Think and Grow Rich" by Napoleon Hill is a classic self-help book published in 1937 that explores the principles and practices of success. The book is based on the author's extensive research on successful people and his interviews with many successful figures of his time, including Henry Ford, Thomas Edison, and Andrew Carnegie.

The book is divided into thirteen chapters that cover a range of topics, including the power of positive thinking, the importance of persistence, the power of belief, the value of goal setting, the role of imagination, and the importance of taking action.

Hill argues that success starts with a clear and specific goal, which is achieved through a combination of focused thoughts, actions, and persistence. He stresses the importance of developing a positive mental attitude and the power of belief, encouraging readers to use their imagination to visualize success and create a clear mental picture of what they want to achieve.

Throughout the book, Hill provides numerous examples of successful people who applied these principles in their lives and achieved great success. He also offers practical advice on how to develop these habits and practices in your own life.

Overall, "Think and Grow Rich" is a powerful and influential book that has inspired millions of readers to develop the mindset and habits necessary to achieve success in their lives. It continues to be a popular and influential book on personal development and success.

2.   The 7 Habits of Highly Effective People by Stephen R. Covey

Quotes

"The key is not to prioritize what's on your schedule, but to schedule your priorities."

"Begin with the end in mind."

"Seek first to understand, then to be understood."

"Synergy is the highest activity of life; it creates new untapped alternatives; it values and exploits the mental, emotional, and psychological differences between people."

"Most people do not listen with the intent to understand; they listen with the intent to reply."

"The most effective way I know to begin with the end in mind is to develop a personal mission statement or philosophy or creed."

"Interdependence is a higher value than independence."

"We are not human beings having a spiritual experience. We are spiritual beings having a human experience."

"There are three constants in life: change, choice and principles."

"You have to decide what your highest priorities are and have the courage pleasantly, smilingly, non-apologetically, to say 'no' to other things. And the way to do that is by having a bigger 'yes' burning inside."

Lessons

Here are some of the key lessons that can be learned from "The 7 Habits of Highly Effective People" by Stephen Covey:

Take responsibility for your life: One of the key messages of the book is that you are in control of your life, and you have the power to choose your actions and responses. Covey emphasizes the importance of being proactive and taking responsibility for your own happiness and success.

Start with the end in mind: Before embarking on any task or project, Covey suggests that you should first envision the desired outcome. By starting with the end in mind, you can create a clear vision of what you want to achieve, and then work backwards to create a plan for getting there.

Prioritize the important over the urgent: Covey suggests that many people get caught up in urgent tasks that demand their attention, but aren't necessarily important. To be truly effective, he recommends that you focus on the important tasks that align with your values and goals, even if they are not urgent.

Seek first to understand, then to be understood: One of the most powerful habits in the book is the fifth habit, which emphasizes the importance of active listening and empathy. By seeking to understand others' perspectives, you can build stronger relationships and make better decisions.

Think win-win: Covey encourages readers to adopt a mindset of cooperation and collaboration, rather than competition. By seeking mutually beneficial solutions and looking for ways to help others succeed, you can create win-win outcomes that benefit everyone.

Synergize: Another key habit is the sixth habit, which encourages people to work together to achieve shared goals. By leveraging the strengths of others and working collaboratively, you can create something greater than the sum of its parts.

Summary

"The 7 Habits of Highly Effective People" is a self-help book written by Stephen R. Covey, first published in 1989. The book aims to provide readers with practical and effective strategies for personal and professional development.

The book is organized into seven main habits that Covey identifies as critical to achieving success and happiness in life. These habits are:

Be proactive: Take responsibility for your actions and choices and focus on things you can control.

Begin with the end in mind: Define your goals and priorities and work towards them consistently.

Put first things first: Prioritize your tasks and focus on the most important and urgent ones.

Think win-win: Aim for mutually beneficial solutions in your relationships and interactions.

Seek first to understand, then to be understood: Listen to others and seek to understand their perspective before sharing your own.

Synergize: Work collaboratively with others to achieve shared goals and create synergy.

Sharpen the saw: Continuously improve yourself through personal and professional development.

Covey emphasizes the importance of developing a strong sense of personal character and values, as well as cultivating strong relationships with others. He also emphasizes the importance of aligning personal and professional goals with a larger sense of purpose and meaning.

Overall, "The 7 Habits of Highly Effective People" is a classic self-help book that offers practical advice and strategies for personal and professional growth. Covey's seven habits provide a framework for achieving success and happiness by focusing on personal responsibility, effective communication, and collaboration with others.

Continuously improve: The seventh habit, "sharpen the saw," emphasizes the importance of self-care and personal development. Covey suggests that to be truly effective, you must constantly work on improving yourself in all areas of your life, including physical, mental, emotional, and spiritual well-being.

Overall, "The 7 Habits of Highly Effective People" offers valuable insights and practical strategies for living a more fulfilling and successful life. By adopting these habits and principles, readers can improve their personal and professional lives and achieve their goals with greater ease and satisfaction.

3.   How to Win Friends and Influence People by Dale Carnegie

Quotes

"You can make more friends in two months by becoming interested in other people than you can in two years by trying to get other people interested in you."

"The only way to get the best of an argument is to avoid it."

"When dealing with people, let us remember we are not dealing with creatures of logic. We are dealing with creatures of emotion, creatures bristling with prejudices and motivated by pride and vanity."

"Success in dealing with people depends on a sympathetic grasp of the other person's viewpoint."

"Remember that a person's name is to that person the sweetest and most important sound in any language."

"Any fool can criticize, condemn, and complain, but it takes character and self-control to be understanding and forgiving."

"If you want others to like you, if you want to develop real friendships, if you want to help others at the same time as you help yourself, keep this principle in mind: become genuinely interested in other people."

"The royal road to a person's heart is to talk about the things he or she treasures most."

"You can make more friends in a week by being interested in them than you can in a year by trying to get them interested in you."

"The only way on earth to influence other people is to talk about what they want and show them how to get it."

Lessons

"How to Win Friends and Influence People" is a timeless classic written by Dale Carnegie, which provides practical tips on how to become a better communicator and build stronger relationships with others. Here are some key lessons from the book:

Show genuine interest in others: To win friends, you need to show interest in others. Ask questions about their interests, opinions, and experiences, and listen actively to what they have to say.

Smile: A smile is a powerful tool that can break down barriers and create a positive first impression. A genuine smile conveys warmth, openness, and sincerity.

Use people's names: People love to hear their names, and using someone's name is a simple but effective way to make them feel valued and important.

Avoid criticism and condemnation: Criticizing and condemning others will only lead to defensiveness and resentment. Instead, focus on finding common ground and building a rapport based on mutual respect.

Give honest and sincere appreciation: People crave recognition and appreciation for their efforts. When you give honest and sincere appreciation, you create a positive environment that motivates people to do their best.

Be a good listener: Being a good listener is key to effective communication. Pay attention to what the other person is saying, and respond with empathy and understanding.

Encourage others to talk about themselves: People love to talk about themselves and their experiences. Encourage them to do so by asking open-ended questions and showing genuine interest.

Admit your mistakes: Everyone makes mistakes, and admitting them is a sign of strength and humility. Acknowledge your mistakes and take responsibility for your actions.

Try to see things from the other person's perspective: Empathy is a powerful tool that can help you understand others' viewpoints and build stronger relationships. Try to put yourself in their shoes and see things from their perspective.

Make the other person feel important: Everyone wants to feel important and valued. Make the other person feel important by giving them your undivided attention, showing appreciation for their contributions, and acknowledging their accomplishments.

Overall, "How to Win Friends and Influence People" teaches us that effective communication and building strong relationships are key to success in both personal and professional life. By following the principles outlined in the book, we can become better communicators, build stronger relationships, and achieve our goals.

Summary

"How to Win Friends and Influence People" by Dale Carnegie is a self-help book that provides practical advice for developing interpersonal skills and building strong relationships. It was first published in 1936 and has since become a classic in the genre.

The book is divided into four parts, each of which covers a different aspect of interpersonal communication and relationship-building. Part one is focused on fundamental techniques for dealing with people, such as avoiding criticism, giving sincere appreciation, and becoming genuinely interested in others. Part two covers ways to increase your influence and persuade others, including the importance of letting the other person feel like they have won and how to appeal to people's self-interest.

Part three discusses how to win people to your way of thinking, including how to arouse in the other person an eager want and how to be a good listener. Part four covers leadership skills, including how to lead people without causing resentment, how to criticize without creating offense, and how to encourage others to achieve their potential.

Throughout the book, Carnegie uses real-life examples and anecdotes to illustrate his points and make them more accessible. He emphasizes the importance of empathy, positive reinforcement, and building relationships based on mutual respect and understanding. Overall, "How to Win Friends and Influence People" is a practical guide for anyone looking to improve their communication skills and build strong relationships in their personal and professional lives.

4. The Power of Positive Thinking by Norman Vincent Peale

Quotes

"Change your thoughts and you change your world."

"Believe in yourself! Have faith in your abilities! Without a humble but reasonable confidence in your own powers you cannot be successful or happy."

"Formulate and stamp indelibly on your mind a mental picture of yourself as succeeding. Hold this picture tenaciously. Never permit it to fade. Your mind will seek to develop the picture."

"When you expect the best, you release a magnetic force in your mind which by a law of attraction tends to bring the best to you."

"The way to happiness: Keep your heart free from hate, your mind from worry. Live simply, expect little, give much. Fill your life with love. Scatter sunshine. Forget self, think of others. Do as you would be done by."

"The life of inner peace, being harmonious and without stress, is the easiest type of existence."

"The person who sends out positive thoughts activates the world around him positively and draws back to himself positive results."

"Positive thinking will let you do everything better than negative thinking will."

"Believe in yourself! Have faith in your abilities! Without a humble but reasonable confidence in your own powers, you cannot be successful or happy."

"Stand up to your obstacles and do something about them. You will find that they haven't half the strength you think they have."

Lessons

Norman Vincent Peale's book "The Power of Positive Thinking" is a classic self-help book that teaches readers how to use positive thinking to improve their lives. Here are some of the top lessons learned from the book:

The power of positive thinking: Peale emphasizes the importance of positive thinking and its ability to transform our lives. He encourages readers to cultivate a positive mindset, to believe in themselves, and to focus on their strengths and abilities.

Visualization: Peale advocates the use of visualization as a powerful tool for achieving success. He advises readers to picture themselves achieving their goals and to imagine the steps they need to take to get there.

Faith: Peale's book has a strong religious undertone, and he stresses the importance of faith in overcoming obstacles and achieving success. He encourages readers to have faith in themselves, in God, and in the power of positive thinking.

Persistence: Peale emphasizes the importance of persistence and perseverance in achieving our goals. He encourages readers to keep trying, even in the face of setbacks and challenges, and to learn from their mistakes.

Action: Peale emphasizes that positive thinking alone is not enough to achieve success. He encourages readers to take action, to set goals, and to develop a plan to achieve them.

Self-improvement: Peale stresses the importance of continuous self-improvement. He encourages readers to identify their weaknesses and to work on improving them, while also focusing on their strengths and building on them.

Gratitude: Peale encourages readers to develop an attitude of gratitude, to appreciate the blessings in their lives, and to focus on the positive aspects of their experiences.

Overall, "The Power of Positive Thinking" teaches readers to cultivate a positive mindset, to have faith in themselves and in the power of positive thinking, and to take action to achieve their goals.

Summary

"The Power of Positive Thinking" is a self-help book written by Norman Vincent Peale that was first published in 1952. The book focuses on the power of positive thinking and how it can help individuals achieve success and happiness in their lives.

The book is divided into 20 chapters, each of which explores different aspects of positive thinking. Peale starts by introducing the concept of positive thinking and explaining how it can transform one's life. He then goes on to discuss the importance of faith and how it can help individuals overcome obstacles and achieve their goals.

Throughout the book, Peale provides practical tips and strategies for developing a positive attitude and outlook on life. He encourages readers to use affirmations, visualization, and other techniques to reprogram their minds and overcome negative thinking patterns.

Peale also emphasizes the importance of taking action and putting positive thinking into practice. He provides examples of successful individuals who have used positive thinking to achieve their goals, and he encourages readers to believe in themselves and their abilities.

Overall, "The Power of Positive Thinking" is a classic self-help book that has helped millions of people improve their lives. It is a timeless reminder that a positive attitude and outlook can make all the difference in achieving success and happiness.

5. Awaken the Giant Within by Tony Robbins

Quotes

"The path to success is to take massive, determined action."

"It's not the events of our lives that shape us, but our beliefs as to what those events mean."

"Beliefs have the power to create and the power to destroy. Human beings have the awesome ability to take any experience of their lives and create a meaning that disempowers them or one that can literally save their lives."

"The quality of your life is the quality of your relationships."

"If you want to be successful, find someone who has achieved the results you want and copy what they do and you'll achieve the same results."

"The only limit to your impact is your imagination and commitment."

"Success is buried on the other side of rejection."

"The secret of success is learning how to use pain and pleasure instead of having pain and pleasure use you."

"There's always a way - if you're committed."

"Your past does not equal your future."

Lessons

Take control of your emotions: Our emotions play a powerful role in shaping our actions and behavior. By learning to take control of our emotional responses, we can make better decisions and take purposeful actions towards our goals.

Identify and change limiting beliefs: Our beliefs can either support us or hold us back from achieving our goals. By identifying and changing limiting beliefs, we can unlock our full potential and create the life we desire.

Define your values: Our values guide our actions and behavior. By identifying and prioritizing our values, we can make decisions that align with our true desires and lead to a more fulfilling life.

Create a compelling vision: Having a clear and compelling vision for our future can motivate us towards our goals and give us a sense of purpose and direction.

Take massive action: Success requires taking massive action towards our goals. By breaking down our goals into smaller, manageable steps and consistently taking action, we can make progress towards our desired outcomes.

Cultivate positive relationships: The quality of our relationships can have a significant impact on our overall well-being and success. By cultivating positive, supportive relationships with others, we can lead a more fulfilling life.

Embrace discomfort: Change and growth require discomfort and effort. By embracing discomfort and pushing ourselves out of our comfort zones, we can achieve our goals and live a more fulfilling life.

Overall, "Awaken the Giant Within" provides valuable insights and practical strategies for transforming our lives and achieving success. By implementing these lessons, readers can overcome limiting beliefs, take control of their emotions, and create a life that aligns with their values and desires.

Summary

"Awaken the Giant Within" by Tony Robbins is a self-help book that provides readers with practical strategies for transforming their lives and achieving success. The book focuses on the power of the mind and how our beliefs, emotions, and behaviors shape our lives.

Throughout the book, Robbins emphasizes the importance of taking control of our emotions, identifying and changing limiting beliefs, defining our values, creating a compelling vision for our future, and taking massive action towards our goals. He also discusses the importance of cultivating positive relationships and embracing discomfort in order to achieve growth and change.

The book provides readers with actionable steps and exercises to implement these strategies in their own lives. It emphasizes the power of the mind and the ability to overcome obstacles and achieve success by tapping into our inner potential.

Overall, "Awaken the Giant Within" is a valuable resource for anyone looking to transform their life and achieve their goals. By implementing the strategies outlined in the book, readers can unlock their full potential and create a life that aligns with their values and desires.

CHAPTER 2

Goal Setting and Achievement

6. The Magic of Thinking Big by David J. Schwartz

Quotes

"Believe it can be done. When you believe something can be done, really believe, your mind will find the ways to do it."

"The size of your success is measured by the strength of your desire; the size of your dream; and how you handle disappointment along the way."

"Success is determined not by whether or not you face obstacles, but by your reaction to them. And if you look at these obstacles as a containing fence, they become your excuse for failure. If you look at them as a hurdle, each one strengthens you for the next."

"Action cures fear. Indecision, postponement, on the other hand, fertilize fear."

"Think big, act big, and live big."

"When you believe something can be done, your mind will find the ways to do it. Believing a solution paves the way to solution."

"Success is based on action. The successful people keep moving. They make mistakes, but they don't quit."

"The person determined to achieve maximum success learns the principle that progress is made one step at a time. A house is built one brick at a time. Football games are won a play at a time. A department store grows bigger one customer at a time. Every big accomplishment is a series of little accomplishments."

"Excusitis is the failure disease."

"Look at things not as they are, but as they can be."

Lessons

Believe in yourself: One of the central themes of the book is the importance of having a positive attitude and believing in yourself. Schwartz argues that our thoughts and beliefs have a direct impact on our actions and ultimately determine our level of success. By cultivating a positive mindset and believing in ourselves, we can achieve great things.

Set big goals: According to Schwartz, setting ambitious goals is crucial to achieving success. He encourages readers to think big and aim for the highest possible level of achievement. By setting big goals, we can tap into our full potential and achieve extraordinary results.

Take action: Taking action is essential to overcoming fear and achieving our goals. Schwartz emphasizes the importance of taking small steps towards our goals, even if they seem insignificant. By taking action, we can build momentum and overcome obstacles.

Surround yourself with positive influences: Schwartz stresses the importance of surrounding ourselves with positive influences, such as successful and optimistic people. By associating with positive people and exposing ourselves to positive ideas and messages, we can cultivate a positive mindset and achieve success.

Learn from failure: According to Schwartz, failure is a necessary part of the learning process. He encourages readers to view failure as an opportunity to learn and grow, rather than a setback. By learning from our mistakes and adapting our approach, we can achieve greater success in the future.

Take responsibility for your life: Schwartz emphasizes the importance of taking responsibility for our lives and our decisions. He argues that we have the power to shape our lives and our futures, and that we should take ownership of our actions and choices. By taking responsibility, we can overcome excuses and achieve our goals.

Summary

"The Magic of Thinking Big" by David J. Schwartz is a self-help book that offers practical advice and strategies for achieving success in all areas of life. The book emphasizes the importance of having a positive mindset and taking action towards our goals, as well as setting ambitious goals, surrounding ourselves with positive influences, learning from failure, and taking responsibility for our lives.

Schwartz argues that our thoughts and beliefs have a direct impact on our actions and ultimately determine our level of success. He encourages readers to cultivate a positive mindset and believe in themselves, as well as take action towards their goals, even if the steps seem small. Schwartz also stresses the importance of surrounding ourselves with positive influences, such as successful and optimistic people, and learning from failure as an opportunity for growth.

Overall, "The Magic of Thinking Big" offers a comprehensive and practical guide to achieving success and overcoming obstacles in all areas of life, from personal relationships to business and finance.

7. The Compound Effect by Darren Hardy

Quotes

"Small, Smart Choices + Consistency + Time = RADICAL DIFFERENCE"

"You will never change your life until you change something you do daily."

"The compound effect is the principle of reaping huge rewards from a series of small, smart choices."

"Success is not overnight. It's when every day you get a little better than the day before. It all adds up."

"What you do every day matters more than what you do once in a while."

"The real key to lifelong success is the regular exercise of a single emotional muscle: gratitude."

"Your habits will determine your future."

"The right information plus the right habits plus the right daily actions equals success."

"It's not the big things that add up in the end; it's the hundreds, thousands, or millions of little things that separate the ordinary from the extraordinary."

"You don't have to be great to start, but you have to start to be great."

Lessons

Small actions can have big results: Hardy emphasizes the power of making small, consistent actions in order to create meaningful change over time. This means that even small improvements can compound over time to create significant results.

Personal responsibility is key: Hardy stresses that individuals are responsible for their own success and that taking personal responsibility for one's actions is crucial. This means being accountable for the choices made and being willing to make changes in order to achieve one's goals.

Habits are crucial: Developing positive habits is crucial for success according to Hardy. He explains that habits create a momentum of success, allowing individuals to achieve their goals and make progress towards them.

Consistency is key: Consistency is key when it comes to achieving long-term success. Hardy explains that small actions must be performed consistently over time to create the desired results.

It's important to say no: Hardy emphasizes the importance of saying no to distractions and focusing on what is truly important. This means setting priorities and avoiding unnecessary activities that do not align with one's goals.

Continuous improvement is necessary: Hardy believes in the importance of continuously improving oneself and striving for personal growth. This means setting goals, seeking feedback, and making changes in order to become the best version of oneself.

Success is a process, not an event: Hardy believes that success is a process that takes time and effort. This means being patient and committed to the process, even when results are not immediately visible.

Overall, "The Compound Effect" teaches readers that success is achieved through small, consistent actions and personal responsibility. By focusing on positive habits, staying consistent, saying no to distractions, and continuously improving oneself, individuals can achieve their goals and create lasting success.

Summary

"The Compound Effect" by Darren Hardy is a self-help book that focuses on the power of small, consistent actions to create significant results over time. Hardy argues that success is not about making one big change or taking one big action, but rather about making small, smart choices consistently over time. He calls this the "compound effect" and believes that it can be applied to any area of life, from personal development to business success.

Throughout the book, Hardy provides practical advice and actionable strategies for implementing the compound effect in your own life. He emphasizes the importance of taking personal responsibility for your actions and making intentional choices that align with your goals. He also stresses the importance of developing positive habits, building strong relationships, and having a growth mindset.

One of the key messages of the book is that small changes can have a big impact over time. Hardy encourages readers to focus on making small, consistent improvements in their lives rather than looking for quick fixes or instant gratification. He also emphasizes the importance of staying focused and avoiding distractions, saying no to things that do not align with your goals, and constantly seeking to improve yourself.

Overall, "The Compound Effect" is a motivational and practical guide to achieving success in any area of life. By making small, smart choices consistently over time, readers can create a momentum of success that will carry them to their goals.

8. The One Thing by Gary Keller and Jay Papasan

Quotes

"Success is about doing the right thing, not about doing everything right."

"The key to success is figuring out your one thing, and then focusing on it with everything you've got."

"Extraordinary results are directly determined by how narrow you can make your focus."

"When you want the absolute best chance to succeed at anything you want, your approach should always be the same. Go small."

"The only way to get where you want to go is to get on the right track, and stay there."

"Multitasking is a lie."

"When you try to be everything to everyone, you inevitably end up being nothing to anyone."

"You can do two things at once, but you can't focus effectively on two things at once."

"The path of mastering something is the combination of not only doing the best you can do at it, but also doing it the best it can be done."

"Success is sequential, not simultaneous. No one actually has the discipline to acquire more than one powerful new habit at a time."

Lessons

Identify your most important task: In order to achieve success, it is important to identify your most important task and focus your time and energy on that. By focusing on one thing, you can make progress towards your goals in a more effective manner.

Prioritize your time: Not all tasks are equally important. By prioritizing your time and focusing on what matters most, you can achieve more success and make progress towards your goals.

Focus on one thing at a time: Trying to tackle multiple tasks simultaneously can be overwhelming and ultimately lead to decreased productivity. By focusing on one thing at a time, you can achieve more success and make progress towards your goals in a more efficient manner.

Continuously improve: Mastery requires continuous improvement. By striving for excellence and continuously improving, individuals can achieve mastery and ultimately, success.

Embrace the power of small steps: Big goals can be overwhelming. By breaking them down into smaller, more manageable steps, individuals can make progress towards their goals and achieve success in a step-by-step manner.

Eliminate distractions: Distractions can derail progress towards achieving goals. By eliminating distractions and focusing on what matters most, individuals can achieve more success and make progress towards their goals in a more efficient manner.

Use the 80/20 rule: The 80/20 rule suggests that 80% of your results come from 20% of your efforts. By identifying the 20% of your efforts that yield the most results, you can prioritize your time and achieve more success.

Summary

"The One Thing" by Gary Keller and Jay Papasan is a book about achieving success by focusing on one thing at a time. The authors argue that success is achieved through a sequential process and that individuals should identify their most important task and focus on that first, before moving on to other tasks. They suggest that by focusing on one thing, individuals can achieve more success than they would by spreading their attention across multiple tasks. The book also emphasizes the importance of prioritization, continuous improvement, and eliminating distractions. The authors suggest that by embracing the power of small steps and using the 80/20 rule, individuals can achieve more success and make progress towards their goals in a more efficient manner. Overall, "The One Thing" is a practical guide to achieving success by focusing on what matters most.

9. The 12 Week Year by Brian P. Moran and Michael Lennington

Quotes

"Without clarity, you will only work hard at the wrong things."

"Vision without action is merely a dream. Action without vision just passes the time. Vision with action can change the world."

"You can't manage time, but you can manage your focus."

"What gets measured, gets managed."

"Motivation is what gets you started. Habit is what keeps you going."

"A goal without a plan is just a wish."

"Distraction is the enemy of achievement."

"You can have results or excuses, not both."

"Discipline is the bridge between goals and accomplishment."

"Success is not a marathon of life. It is a series of sprints."

Lessons

Short-term goals are more effective than long-term goals. The book argues that people are more likely to achieve their goals when they set shorter time frames, such as 12 weeks, instead of a full year. Short-term goals create a sense of urgency and accountability, which helps people stay focused and motivated.

Focus on a few key goals at a time. The authors recommend focusing on a maximum of three to five key goals during each 12-week year. This helps people avoid overwhelm and stay focused on what's most important.

Set specific, measurable goals. The book emphasizes the importance of setting specific, measurable goals that are tied to a deadline. This helps people stay focused and accountable, and ensures that they are making progress towards their goals.

Prioritize your time. The authors argue that people often waste time on low-value activities that don't contribute to their goals. To be successful, people need to prioritize their time and focus on high-value activities that will help them achieve their goals.

Review progress regularly. The book emphasizes the importance of regularly reviewing progress towards goals, and making adjustments as needed. This helps people stay on track and make course corrections when necessary.

Build accountability into the process. The authors recommend building accountability into the goal-setting process by sharing goals with others and tracking progress towards those goals. This helps people stay motivated and accountable, and can also provide support and encouragement.

Embrace discomfort. The book argues that achieving big goals requires stepping out of one's comfort zone and embracing discomfort. This means being willing to take risks, face challenges, and make sacrifices in order to achieve success.

Overall, "The 12 Week Year" offers a powerful framework for achieving more in a shorter amount of time. By focusing on short-term goals, prioritizing time, and building accountability into the process, people can achieve more than they ever thought possible.

Summary

"The 12 Week Year" by Brian P. Moran and Michael Lennington is a book that presents a framework for achieving more in a shorter amount of time. The book argues that people are more likely to achieve their goals when they focus on shorter time frames, such as 12 weeks, instead of a full year. The authors emphasize the importance of setting specific, measurable goals that are tied to a deadline, prioritizing time, and building accountability into the goal-setting process. The book also emphasizes the importance of regularly reviewing progress towards goals and making adjustments as needed. By following this framework, people can achieve more than they ever thought possible and reach their full potential. Overall, "The 12 Week Year" is a powerful tool for anyone looking to achieve big goals and make significant progress towards their dreams and aspirations.

10. Eat That Frog! by Brian Tracy

Quotes

"The most valuable tasks you can do each day are often the hardest and most complex. But the payoff and rewards for completing these tasks efficiently and effectively can be tremendous."

"Successful people are those who are willing to delay gratification and make sacrifices in the short term so that they can enjoy far greater rewards in the long term."

"The key to success is action. It's not enough to just think about it or talk about it. You need to actually take action."

"Your frog is your biggest, most important task, the one you are most likely to procrastinate on if you don't do something about it."

"There will never be enough time to do everything you have to do."

"There is never enough time to do everything, but there is always enough time to do the most important thing."

"There is a direct relationship between how much you write down your goals and objectives, and how much you accomplish."

"The ability to concentrate single-mindedly on your most important task, to do it well, and to finish it completely, is the key to great success, achievement, respect, status, and happiness in life."

"The more you discipline yourself to use your time well, the happier you will feel, and the better will be the quality of your life in every area."

"The only real limitation on your abilities is the level of your desire."

Lessons

Prioritization is key: One of the most important lessons from Eat That Frog! is the importance of prioritizing your tasks. By focusing on the most important tasks first, you can avoid procrastination and get more done in less time.

Tackle your biggest task first: Tracy emphasizes the importance of tackling your biggest, most important task first thing in the morning. This helps you to gain momentum and motivation, and sets the tone for the rest of your day.

Break tasks down into smaller steps: If a task seems overwhelming or intimidating, Tracy recommends breaking it down into smaller, more manageable steps. This can make it easier to get started and make progress.

Plan your day in advance: To avoid wasting time and ensure that you are making progress towards your goals, Tracy recommends planning your day in advance. This helps you to stay focused and avoid distractions.

Focus on results, not just activity: It's important to focus on achieving results, rather than just being busy or working hard. By setting clear goals and measuring your progress, you can ensure that you are making progress towards your desired outcomes.

Learn to say no: To avoid overcommitting and spreading yourself too thin, it's important to learn to say no to tasks or projects that are not aligned with your goals or priorities.

Continuous learning and improvement: Finally, Tracy emphasizes the importance of continuous learning and improvement. By staying curious and seeking out new knowledge and skills, you can stay ahead of the curve and continue to grow and develop over time.

Summary

Eat That Frog! by Brian Tracy is a self-help book that offers practical advice on how to overcome procrastination and increase productivity. The book's central concept is the idea of "eating the frog," which means tackling your biggest, most important task first thing in the morning. Tracy emphasizes the importance of prioritization, planning, and focusing on results rather than just activity. He also offers strategies for breaking tasks down into smaller steps, learning to say no to non-priority tasks, and using positive self-talk to stay motivated. Throughout the book, Tracy stresses the importance of continuous learning and improvement, and provides practical tips and exercises to help readers implement his strategies in their daily lives. Overall, Eat That Frog! is a valuable resource for anyone who wants to overcome procrastination and achieve greater success and fulfillment in their personal and professional lives.

CHAPTER 3

Time Management and Productivity

11.   Getting Things Done by David Allen

Quotes

"Your mind is for having ideas, not holding them."

"If it's on your mind, your mind isn't clear. Anything you consider unfinished in any way must be captured in a trusted system outside your mind."

"There is no reason ever to have the same thought twice, unless you like having that thought."

"You can do anything, but not everything."

"The more you sweat in peace, the less you bleed in war."

"Your ability to generate power is directly proportional to your ability to relax."

"The real issue is not managing time, but managing ourselves."

"The secret of getting ahead is getting started. The secret of getting started is breaking your complex overwhelming tasks into small manageable tasks, and then starting on the first one."

"It's not enough to be busy, so are the ants. The question is, what are we busy about?"

"The problem is not the problem. The problem is your attitude about the problem."

Lessons

Capture everything: Our brains can only hold a limited amount of information at any given time. To free up mental space, it's essential to capture all our ideas, tasks, and commitments in a trusted system. This can be a notebook, digital app, or any other tool that works for you.

Clarify and organize: Once you've captured all your tasks and commitments, it's essential to clarify what each one involves and organize them in a way that makes sense. This involves asking questions like "What is the next action step?" and "What is the desired outcome?"

Prioritize: Not all tasks are created equal. To be productive, it's important to prioritize your tasks based on their importance and urgency. This can involve using a system like the Eisenhower Matrix to determine which tasks are most important.

Focus on actions, not projects: A project is made up of a series of smaller actions. By focusing on the next action step rather than the entire project, you can make progress and avoid feeling overwhelmed.

Review regularly: To stay on top of your commitments and goals, it's important to review your system regularly. This can involve a weekly review of all your tasks and commitments, as well as daily check-ins to ensure you're staying on track.

Be flexible: No productivity system is perfect, and things will inevitably change. It's important to be flexible and adaptable, adjusting your system as needed to suit your changing needs.

Overall, the lessons from "Getting Things Done" emphasize the importance of having a clear and organized system for managing your tasks and commitments. By capturing everything, clarifying and prioritizing tasks, focusing on actions, and regularly reviewing your system, you can stay productive and achieve your goals.

Summary

"Getting Things Done" by David Allen is a book that provides a system for managing the overwhelming amount of information and tasks that we face in our daily lives. The book presents a step-by-step process for capturing, clarifying, and organizing all of our commitments and responsibilities in a way that allows us to focus on the most important tasks and make progress towards our goals.

The key concepts of the book include the importance of capturing all of our ideas, tasks, and commitments in a trusted system, clarifying what each task involves and organizing them in a way that makes sense, prioritizing tasks based on their importance and urgency, focusing on actions rather than projects, and regularly reviewing our system to stay on top of our commitments and goals.

By following the system outlined in the book, readers can free up mental space, increase productivity, reduce stress and anxiety, and achieve their goals with greater ease and efficiency. Overall, "Getting Things Done" is a practical and actionable guide to managing the complexity of modern life and taking control of our time and productivity.

12.   The 5 AM Club by Robin Sharma

Quotes

"Winning starts at your beginning. And your first hours are where the great heroes are made. Own your mornings and you'll master your life."

"The moment when you first awaken in the morning is the most wonderful of the twenty-four hours. No matter how weary or dreary you may feel, you possess the certainty that, during the day that lies before you, absolutely anything may happen."

"Victims make excuses. Leaders deliver results. Decide what kind of person you want to be."

"The fears you run from run to you."

"In an age of distraction, nothing can feel more luxurious than paying attention."

"To have the results only 5% have, you must be willing to do and think like only 5% do and think."

"Ordinary people love entertainment. Extraordinary people adore education."

"All change is hard at first, messy in the middle and gorgeous at the end."

"The smallest of implementations always trumps the grandest of intentions."

"The key to productivity is simplicity. Time management is dead, in our digital age, attention management is king."

I hope these quotes inspire and motivate you to wake up early and achieve your goals!

Lessons

The power of morning routines: The book emphasizes the importance of waking up early and starting your day with a well-designed morning routine. This can include activities like exercise, meditation, learning, and planning, which can help you boost your productivity, creativity, and overall well-being.

The importance of self-mastery: The book encourages readers to develop the habits and mindset of successful people, including discipline, focus, resilience, and growth mindset. This involves taking ownership of your life, setting clear goals, and investing in your personal development.

The value of lifelong learning: The book stresses the importance of continuous learning and growth, through reading, attending seminars, and seeking out new experiences. This can help you stay curious, adaptable, and innovative, and equip you with the skills and knowledge to achieve your goals.

The role of leadership: The book highlights the importance of leading yourself first, by taking charge of your own life and setting an example for others. It also encourages readers to inspire and empower others, by sharing their knowledge, skills, and resources, and contributing to a greater cause.

The benefits of mindfulness: The book promotes the practice of mindfulness, which involves being present in the moment, non-judgmentally, and with full awareness. This can help you reduce stress, enhance focus, and cultivate a sense of inner peace and well-being.

Overall, "The 5 AM Club" is a comprehensive guide to personal and professional development, offering practical strategies and insights to help readers transform their lives and achieve their full potential.

Summary

"The 5 AM Club" is a self-help book written by Robin Sharma that explores the benefits of waking up early and establishing a morning routine to boost productivity, creativity, and overall well-being. The book follows the journey of four characters - a struggling entrepreneur, a burned-out artist, a corporate executive, and a struggling artist turned entrepreneur - as they meet a mysterious mentor who introduces them to the concept of the 5 AM Club. The mentor teaches them the importance of self-mastery, continuous learning, mindfulness, and leadership, and provides them with practical strategies and tools to help them achieve their goals and transform their lives. The book offers a wealth of insights, advice, and inspirational stories, and is designed to help readers develop the habits, mindset, and skills necessary to succeed in today's fast-paced and competitive world. Overall, "The 5 AM Club" is a comprehensive guide to personal and professional development that provides readers with the tools and inspiration to live a more fulfilling and purposeful life.

13. Deep Work by Cal Newport

Quotes

"The ability to perform deep work is becoming increasingly rare at exactly the same time it is becoming increasingly valuable in our economy. As a consequence, the few who cultivate this skill, and then make it the core of their working life, will thrive."

"A deep work habit, once established, generates a momentum that makes the next session easier."

"To produce at your peak level you need to work for extended periods with full concentration on a single task free from distraction."

"Clarity about what matters provides clarity about what does not."

"The Deep Work Hypothesis: The ability to perform deep work is becoming increasingly rare at exactly the same time it is becoming increasingly valuable in our economy. As a consequence, the few who cultivate this skill, and then make it the core of their working life, will thrive."

"The best moments usually occur when a person's body or mind is stretched to its limits in a voluntary effort to accomplish something difficult and worthwhile."

"Efforts to deepen your focus will struggle if you don't simultaneously wean your mind from a dependence on distraction."

"Deep work is like a superpower in our increasingly competitive twenty-first-century economy."

"Deep work is not some nostalgic affectation of writers and early-twentieth-century philosophers. It's instead a skill that has great value today."

"The ability to concentrate intensely is a skill that must be trained."

Lessons

Deep work is valuable: In our increasingly competitive economy, the ability to focus without distraction on a cognitively demanding task is becoming rare and valuable. By cultivating this skill, you can produce better results in less time and stand out in your field.

Deep work requires intentional practice: You can't expect to dive straight into deep work and be successful at it. You need to practice intentionally and build up your ability to focus over time.

Distraction is the enemy of deep work: In order to achieve deep work, you need to minimize distractions as much as possible. This means avoiding things like social media, email, and other forms of digital communication during your deep work sessions.

Time-blocking is essential: In order to make deep work a consistent habit, you need to block off chunks of time in your schedule specifically for this purpose. This means being intentional about your time and treating deep work as a priority.

Work smarter, not harder: Contrary to popular belief, working longer hours does not necessarily lead to better results. Instead, it's important to work smarter by focusing on deep work and intentionally practicing your ability to concentrate.

Multitasking is a myth: Research has shown that multitasking actually leads to lower productivity and decreased focus. Instead, it's better to focus on one task at a time and give it your full attention.

Mindfulness can help with deep work: Mindfulness practices like meditation can help you build your ability to focus and reduce distractions. By training your mind to stay in the present moment, you can improve your ability to concentrate on deep work.

Deep work is a valuable life skill: Even if you don't work in a field that requires deep work, cultivating this skill can have a positive impact on your life as a whole. By learning to focus and be present in the moment, you can improve your relationships, reduce stress, and live a more fulfilling life.

Summary

"Deep Work" by Cal Newport is a book that explores the value and importance of being able to focus deeply on cognitively demanding tasks. Newport argues that in today's knowledge economy, the ability to perform deep work is becoming increasingly rare and valuable. By cultivating this skill, individuals can produce better results in less time and stand out in their field.

The book provides practical advice and strategies for building the habit of deep work, including time-blocking, avoiding distractions, and intentionally practicing your ability to concentrate. Newport also challenges popular notions of multitasking and working longer hours, arguing that working smarter, not harder, is the key to success.

Overall, "Deep Work" is a call to action for individuals to take control of their ability to focus and develop the valuable life skill of deep work. Whether you work in a field that requires deep work or simply want to improve your ability to focus and be present in the moment, this book provides valuable insights and strategies for achieving success.

14. Essentialism: The Disciplined Pursuit of Less by Greg McKeown

Quotes

"The way of the Essentialist means living by design, not by default."

"Essentialism is not about how to get more things done; it's about how to get the right things done."

"The ability to choose cannot be taken away or even given away—it can only be forgotten."

"Essentialists spend as much time as possible exploring, listening, debating, questioning, and thinking. But their exploration is not an end in itself."

"The undisciplined pursuit of more always leads to less."

"If it isn't a clear yes, then it's a clear no."

"We often think of choice as a thing. But a choice is not a thing. Our options may be things, but a choice—a choice is an action."

"We can try to avoid the reality of trade-offs, but we can't escape them."

"The Essentialist doesn't just recognize the power of choice, he celebrates it. The Essentialist knows that when we surrender our right to choose, we give others not just the power but also the explicit permission to choose for us."

"When we really delve into the reasons for why we can't let something go, there are only two: an attachment to the past or a fear for the future."

Lessons

Focus on the essential. In order to achieve maximum productivity and success, it's essential to focus on the things that truly matter. By prioritizing the essential and eliminating the non-essential, we can streamline our lives and work more efficiently.

Embrace the power of choice. We always have the power to choose how we spend our time and energy. By being mindful and intentional about our choices, we can avoid getting pulled in different directions and stay focused on what matters most.

Say no more often. Saying no is an essential skill for the essentialist. By learning to say no to non-essential activities and distractions, we can free up time and energy to focus on what truly matters.

Learn to let go. Sometimes, letting go of non-essential tasks, projects, or commitments can be difficult. But by learning to let go and delegating tasks to others, we can avoid burnout and focus on the things that truly matter.

Prioritize self-care. Taking care of ourselves is an essential aspect of living a fulfilling life. By prioritizing self-care activities such as exercise, meditation, and spending time with loved ones, we can recharge our batteries and stay focused on our goals.

Create a clear vision. Having a clear sense of purpose and direction is essential for achieving success. By creating a clear vision of what we want to achieve, we can stay focused and avoid getting sidetracked by distractions.

Be mindful of trade-offs. Every decision we make comes with trade-offs. By being mindful of these trade-offs and choosing wisely, we can avoid regrets and live a more fulfilling life.

Pursue excellence, not perfection. Perfectionism can be a trap that prevents us from achieving our goals. Instead of striving for perfection, the essentialist focuses on pursuing excellence and making progress toward their goals.

Practice essentialism in all areas of life. Essentialism is not just a business or work philosophy; it can be applied to all areas of life. By prioritizing the essential and eliminating the non-essential, we can live a more meaningful and fulfilling life.

Remember that less is more. The essentialist understands that less is often more. By simplifying our lives and focusing on what truly matters, we can achieve more with less effort and live a more fulfilling life.

Summary

Essentialism: The Disciplined Pursuit of Less by Greg McKeown is a book that encourages readers to focus on what's truly important in their lives and eliminate distractions that prevent them from achieving their goals. The book argues that by prioritizing the essential, we can achieve maximum productivity and success. The author offers practical advice for applying essentialism to various aspects of life, including work, personal relationships, and self-care.

The book emphasizes the importance of saying no to non-essential activities and distractions, learning to let go of non-essential tasks, and delegating responsibilities to others. It also emphasizes the importance of prioritizing self-care activities such as exercise, meditation, and spending time with loved ones. The author encourages readers to create a clear vision of what they want to achieve and to be mindful of the trade-offs that come with every decision.

Overall, the book argues that less is often more and that by simplifying our lives and focusing on what truly matters, we can achieve more with less effort and live a more fulfilling life. It encourages readers to practice essentialism in all areas of life, not just in their work or business pursuits.

15. Atomic Habits by James Clear

Quotes

"Habits are the compound interest of self-improvement."

"Every action you take is a vote for the type of person you wish to become."

"If you're having trouble changing your habits, the problem isn't you. The problem is your system."

"The most effective way to change your habits is to focus not on what you want to achieve, but on who you wish to become."

"You do not rise to the level of your goals. You fall to the level of your systems."

"Habits are the building blocks of any system for getting what you want."

"Habits are like the atoms of our lives. Each one is a fundamental unit that contributes to your overall improvement."

"Small changes often appear to make no difference until you cross a critical threshold. The most powerful outcomes of any compounding process are delayed."

"Habits are a double-edged sword. They can work for you or against you, which is why understanding the details is essential."

"The only way to become excellent is to be endlessly fascinated by doing the same thing over and over."

I hope these quotes inspire you to develop good habits and systems that will help you achieve your goals!

Lessons

Small habits lead to big changes: The book emphasizes the importance of focusing on small, daily habits that contribute to larger goals. Even tiny improvements in your habits can compound over time and lead to significant improvements in your life.

Identity shapes behavior: Clear argues that if you want to change your behavior, you need to first change your identity. By focusing on becoming the type of person who embodies the habits you want to adopt, you can make lasting changes to your behavior.

The power of environment: Our environment has a significant impact on our habits. By making intentional changes to our surroundings, we can make it easier to adopt good habits and break bad ones.

Habits are a process, not a destination: Habits are not just something you do for a short period of time, but rather a way of life. To see lasting changes in your life, you need to adopt habits that you can sustain over the long term.

The importance of tracking progress: Clear stresses the importance of tracking your progress towards your goals. By measuring your progress, you can see the small improvements you're making and stay motivated to continue.

The role of motivation: Motivation is not enough to sustain habits over the long term. Instead, you need to create systems and routines that make it easy to stick with your habits even when motivation is low.

The power of small wins: Celebrating small wins along the way can help you stay motivated and build momentum towards larger goals. Even small victories can be meaningful and keep you on track towards your larger objectives.

The impact of accountability: Having someone to hold you accountable can be a powerful motivator to stick with your habits. Whether it's a friend, coach, or mentor, having someone to report to can help you stay on track and make progress towards your goals.

Overall, the book Atomic Habits provides practical advice for creating lasting changes in your life by focusing on small, daily habits. By adopting a growth mindset and taking intentional action towards your goals, you can build the habits and systems you need to achieve success.

Summary

Atomic Habits by James Clear is a practical guide to building good habits and breaking bad ones. Clear emphasizes the importance of focusing on small, daily habits that contribute to larger goals. He argues that if you want to change your behavior, you need to first change your identity and become the type of person who embodies the habits you want to adopt.

Clear also stresses the importance of creating an environment that supports your habits and routines. By making intentional changes to your surroundings, you can make it easier to adopt good habits and break bad ones. He also provides practical advice for tracking your progress, staying motivated, and building momentum towards your goals.

The book is divided into four parts: The Fundamentals, The Four Laws of Behavior Change, Make It Obvious, and Make It Stick. In each section, Clear provides actionable strategies and real-world examples to help readers build better habits and achieve their goals.

Overall, Atomic Habits is a valuable resource for anyone looking to make lasting changes in their life. The book provides a clear and practical roadmap for building good habits and breaking bad ones, and emphasizes the importance of taking small, consistent actions towards your goals.

CHAPTER 4

Leadership and Management

16.   Good to Great by Jim Collins

Quotes

"Good is the enemy of great."

"Greatness is not a function of circumstance. Greatness, it turns out, is largely a matter of conscious choice and discipline."

"When we begin to reflect and ask how we might contribute to something larger than ourselves, we enter into the realm of leadership."

"The good-to-great leaders never wanted to become larger-than-life heroes. They never aspired to be put on a pedestal or become unreachable icons. They were seemingly ordinary people quietly producing extraordinary results."

"The most successful companies are those that are able to attract and retain self-motivated people who are willing to go the extra mile."

"A culture of discipline is not just about the individual disciplines themselves, but about how they interact."

"Good-to-great companies think differently about the role of technology."

"The hedgehog concept represents the intersection of three circles: What you are deeply passionate about, What you can be the best in the world at, and What drives your economic engine."

"A great piece of art is composed not just of what is in the final piece, but equally important, what is not. It is the discipline to discard what does not fit – to cut out what might have already cost days or even years of effort – that distinguishes the truly exceptional artist and marks the ideal piece of work, be it a symphony, a novel, a painting, a company or, most important of all, a life."

"The signature of mediocrity is not an unwillingness to change; the signature of mediocrity is chronic inconsistency."

Lessons

Level 5 Leadership: One of the key characteristics of a great company is having a Level 5 leader. These leaders are humble, selfless, and have a fierce ambition for the success of the company rather than themselves.

First Who, Then What: Great companies first focus on getting the right people on the bus, and then figure out where to go. This means finding and hiring the right people who are committed to the company's vision and values before deciding on a specific direction.

Confront the Brutal Facts: In order to succeed, great companies must be willing to confront the brutal facts about their current reality. This means acknowledging weaknesses and facing challenges head-on, rather than ignoring or denying them.

The Hedgehog Concept: The most successful companies have a clear understanding of their "hedgehog concept," which is the intersection of their passion, skills, and economic opportunities. This helps them focus on what they can be the best in the world at and avoid spreading themselves too thin.

Culture of Discipline: Great companies have a culture of discipline, which means they have a clear understanding of what they should and should not be doing, and they have the discipline to stick to their goals and avoid distractions.

Technology Accelerators, Not Drivers: Great companies use technology as a tool to accelerate their progress, rather than allowing it to drive their strategy. They focus on what they are good at and use technology to enhance their strengths.

The Flywheel Effect: Great companies build momentum slowly over time, like a flywheel, by consistently making small improvements that compound over time. This allows them to sustain long-term success and outperform their competitors.

Overall, "Good to Great" teaches us that achieving greatness is possible for any company, as long as they have the right leadership, team, strategy, and culture of discipline. By focusing on these key areas and continually making small improvements, any company can reach their full potential and become truly great.

Summary

"Good to Great" by Jim Collins is a business book that explores why some companies are able to achieve long-term success and become great, while others remain merely good or even fail. Collins and his research team analyzed a group of 28 companies that made the transition from good to great over a 15-year period, and compared them to a control group of companies that remained average. Through this research, Collins identified several key characteristics that distinguished great companies from good ones.

The book outlines the findings of this research and presents a framework for achieving long-term greatness. The key concepts include the importance of having Level 5 leadership, the need to get the right people on the bus before deciding on a specific direction, the importance of confronting the brutal facts about the company's current reality, and the need to focus on the company's "hedgehog concept" to avoid spreading the company too thin.

Collins also emphasizes the importance of building a culture of discipline and using technology as an accelerator rather than a driver of strategy. Finally, he discusses the "flywheel effect," which is the idea that great companies build momentum slowly over time, like a flywheel, by consistently making small improvements that compound over time.

Overall, "Good to Great" provides a comprehensive and research-based approach to achieving long-term success and becoming a great company. By following the key principles outlined in the book, any company can increase its chances of achieving greatness and sustaining it over the long term.

17.   The Lean Startup by Eric Ries

Quotes

"A startup is a human institution designed to create something new under conditions of extreme uncertainty."

"The only way to win is to learn faster than anyone else."

"Validated learning is the process of demonstrating empirically that a team has discovered valuable truths about a startup's present and future business prospects."

"The goal of a startup is to figure out the right thing to build—the thing customers want and will pay for—as quickly as possible."

"The product roadmap is a living document. It's not a contract, nor is it a feature delivery schedule. It is a tool to help you visualize and share the direction of your product with your team and the rest of the organization."

"A minimum viable product (MVP) is that version of a new product which allows a team to collect the maximum amount of validated learning about customers with the least effort."

"By measuring learning instead of time, we can accurately predict progress."

"The only way to know if an idea is good is to take it to the customers."

"Entrepreneurship is management."

"The greatest waste in the world is the difference between what we are and what we could become."

Lessons

Embrace uncertainty: Startups operate in conditions of extreme uncertainty, and the key to success is to embrace this uncertainty and continually test and learn from the market.

Focus on validated learning: Validated learning involves using data to demonstrate that a team has discovered valuable truths about a startup's present and future business prospects. It is important to focus on validated learning to make informed decisions.

Build a minimum viable product (MVP): The MVP is the simplest version of a new product that allows a team to collect the maximum amount of validated learning about customers with the least effort. Building an MVP enables startups to test their ideas and validate them with real customers.

Measure progress: Measuring progress is important for startups, but it's important to measure the right things. Instead of measuring time, startups should focus on measuring validated learning to accurately predict progress.

Pivot when necessary: Startups need to be flexible and willing to pivot when they encounter new information or changes in the market. It's important to be willing to change course when necessary to stay relevant and competitive.

Continuous innovation: Continuous innovation is critical for startups to stay ahead of the competition. By constantly testing and learning from the market, startups can continue to improve their products and services to meet customer needs.

Entrepreneurship is management: The Lean Startup approach emphasizes the importance of managing a startup like a business. This means setting goals, measuring progress, and making data-driven decisions based on validated learning.

Overall, the book emphasizes the importance of taking an iterative, data-driven approach to entrepreneurship, focusing on customer needs, and being willing to pivot and adapt as necessary to achieve success.

Summary

The Lean Startup by Eric Ries is a book about entrepreneurship and how to build successful businesses in conditions of extreme uncertainty. The book advocates for an iterative, data-driven approach to entrepreneurship, where startups continually test and learn from the market to build products that customers want and are willing to pay for.

Ries introduces the concept of the minimum viable product (MVP), which is the simplest version of a new product that allows a team to collect the maximum amount of validated learning about customers with the least effort. By building an MVP and continually testing and iterating on the product, startups can quickly learn what works and what doesn't, and make informed decisions about how to proceed.

The book also emphasizes the importance of focusing on validated learning, rather than simply measuring progress based on time or other metrics. Startups need to be flexible and willing to pivot when they encounter new information or changes in the market, and they need to be continuously innovating to stay ahead of the competition.

Throughout the book, Ries provides real-world examples and case studies to illustrate his points, and he also offers practical advice for how to apply the Lean Startup approach to a wide range of businesses and industries. Overall, The Lean Startup offers a compelling and actionable framework for building successful businesses in today's rapidly changing market.

18.   Start with Why by Simon Sinek

Quotes

"People don't buy what you do; they buy why you do it."

"Leadership requires two things: a vision of the world that does not yet exist and the ability to communicate it."

"There are only two ways to influence human behavior: you can manipulate it or you can inspire it."

"If you hire people just because they can do a job, they'll work for your money. But if you hire people who believe what you believe, they'll work for you with blood and sweat and tears."

"The goal is not to do business with everyone who needs what you have. The goal is to do business with people who believe what you believe."

"When people are financially invested, they want a return. When people are emotionally invested, they want to contribute."

"Great leaders are willing to sacrifice their own personal interests for the good of the team."

"Working hard for something we don't care about is called stress; working hard for something we love is called passion."

"The best organizations are the ones in which everyone is not only encouraged to contribute but also feels safe enough to do so."

"An organization's values define it; they shape the way it operates and they define its character."

Lessons

Purpose is essential: A clear and inspiring sense of purpose is vital to creating a successful organization. The most successful companies are not just focused on what they do, but also on why they do it.

Start with why: To build a successful organization, you must start with why. You must have a clear sense of purpose and be able to communicate it effectively to your employees and customers.

Understand your audience: To effectively communicate your why, you must understand your audience. You must know what they believe in and what motivates them.

Leadership matters: Leadership plays a critical role in setting the tone and culture of an organization. Great leaders inspire their employees and lead by example.

Create a culture of trust: Trust is essential to building a successful organization. Leaders must create a culture of trust by being transparent and consistent in their actions.

Empower your employees: Employees who feel valued and empowered are more engaged and committed to their work. Leaders must create an environment where employees feel safe to share their ideas and take risks.

Focus on the long-term: Building a successful organization takes time and patience. Leaders must focus on the long-term and be willing to make sacrifices to achieve their goals.

Embrace failure: Failure is a necessary part of the learning process. Leaders must embrace failure and encourage their employees to take risks and learn from their mistakes.

Stay true to your values: Organizations that stay true to their values and beliefs are more likely to succeed in the long-term. Leaders must ensure that their actions align with their values and that they are always striving to live up to their ideals.

Keep learning: Learning is a lifelong process. Leaders must be open to new ideas and be willing to continuously learn and grow.

Summary

In "Start with Why," Simon Sinek explores the idea that successful organizations and leaders are those who start with why they do what they do, rather than focusing solely on what they do or how they do it. He argues that a clear and inspiring sense of purpose is essential for building a successful organization, and that great leaders are those who are able to communicate this purpose to their employees and customers.

Sinek provides numerous examples of companies and individuals who have successfully built their organizations around their sense of purpose, and shows how these organizations have been able to achieve exceptional results. He also discusses the importance of leadership in setting the tone and culture of an organization, and how leaders must create a culture of trust, empowerment, and learning in order to succeed.

Overall, "Start with Why" emphasizes the importance of purpose and values in building a successful organization, and provides practical advice and insights for leaders who want to create a culture of inspiration, innovation, and growth.

19. The 21 Irrefutable Laws of Leadership by John C. Maxwell

Quotes

"Leadership is not about titles, positions or flowcharts. It is about one life influencing another."

"The true test of leadership is how well you function in a crisis."

"The leader's attitude is like a thermostat for the workplace. If the leader is enthusiastic and positive, the morale of the team will reflect that. If the leader is negative and pessimistic, the team will respond in kind."

"The mark of a great leader is not necessarily how many followers they have, but how many leaders they create."

"People don't care how much you know until they know how much you care."

"Leadership is not about being in charge. It is about taking care of those in your charge."

"To lead yourself, use your head; to lead others, use your heart."

"The best leaders are the ones most willing to surround themselves with people smarter than they are."

"The greatest leaders mobilize others by coalescing people around a shared vision."

"Leadership is not a destination, but a journey. It is the process of continually learning, growing, and improving."

"Leadership is influence, nothing more, nothing less."

"The most effective way to lead is to lead by example."

"A good leader is a person who takes a little more than his share of the blame and a little less than his share of the credit."

"The key to successful leadership today is influence, not authority."

"The best leaders are always the best learners."

"Leadership develops daily, not in a day."

"You don't have to be great to start, but you have to start to be great."

"Leadership is not about what you do, but about who you are and how you influence others."

"The difference between a boss and a leader: a boss says, 'Go!' - a leader says, 'Let's go!'"

"Leadership is about creating an environment where people can bring their best selves to work every day."

"The greatest enemy of good thinking is busyness."

Lessons

There are many valuable lessons to be learned from "The 21 Irrefutable Laws of Leadership" by John C. Maxwell. Here are some of the key lessons that can be gleaned from the book:

Leadership is a skill that can be learned and developed over time. While some people may have natural leadership abilities, anyone can improve their leadership skills through practice and education.

Effective leaders are those who are willing to take risks and make difficult decisions. They are not afraid to fail and are always looking for ways to improve.

Leaders must have a clear vision and be able to communicate that vision to others. They must also be able to inspire and motivate others to work towards that vision.

Leaders must be able to build strong relationships with their followers. They must be able to earn their trust and respect and be willing to listen to their ideas and concerns.

Leaders must be willing to lead by example. They must model the behavior they want to see in others and be willing to roll up their sleeves and get their hands dirty.

Successful leaders are those who are willing to learn from their mistakes and use those lessons to improve their leadership skills.

Leaders must be adaptable and willing to change their approach when necessary. They must also be able to anticipate and prepare for future challenges.

Leaders must be able to delegate effectively. They must be able to identify the strengths and weaknesses of their team members and assign tasks accordingly.

Leaders must be able to maintain a positive attitude and remain optimistic, even in the face of adversity.

Finally, effective leaders are those who are able to inspire and empower others to become leaders themselves. They recognize that leadership is not about holding power over others, but about creating a shared vision and working together to achieve it.

Summary

"The 21 Irrefutable Laws of Leadership" by John C. Maxwell is a book that outlines 21 principles of leadership that are essential for anyone who wants to become an effective leader. Maxwell argues that leadership is a skill that can be learned and developed over time, and that the most successful leaders are those who are willing to take risks, communicate their vision, build strong relationships, lead by example, and adapt to changing circumstances.

The book is divided into 21 chapters, each of which focuses on a different "law" of leadership. These laws include things like the Law of Influence (which states that leadership is about influence, nothing more, nothing less), the Law of Process (which emphasizes that leadership is a journey, not a destination), and the Law of Navigation (which emphasizes the importance of setting a course and having a plan).

Throughout the book, Maxwell uses examples from history and his own experiences to illustrate each of these laws and show how they can be applied in a variety of different settings. He also includes practical exercises and questions at the end of each chapter to help readers apply the lessons to their own lives and leadership roles.

Overall, "The 21 Irrefutable Laws of Leadership" is a comprehensive guide to leadership that is filled with practical advice, real-world examples, and inspiring stories. Whether you're a CEO, a manager, or just someone who wants to become a better leader in any area of your life, this book is an essential resource.

20. First Things First by Stephen Covey, A. Roger Merrill, and Rebecca R. Merrill

Quotes

"The main thing is to keep the main thing the main thing."

"The key is not to prioritize what's on your schedule, but to schedule your priorities."

"It's not enough to be busy, so are the ants. The question is, what are we busy about?"

"The enemy of the 'best' is often the 'good.'"

"We often become so busy making a living that we forget to make a life."

"The most important thing you can do to achieve your goals is to make sure that as soon as you set them, you immediately begin to create momentum."

"The way we spend our time defines who we are."

"The only limits on your life are those that you set yourself."

"The challenge is not to manage time, but to manage ourselves."

"The key is not to do more things, but to do the right things."

Lessons

Prioritize what truly matters: To live a fulfilling and meaningful life, it is important to prioritize what truly matters to us. This involves identifying our core values and aligning our activities with those values. By doing so, we can ensure that we are spending our time and energy on the things that truly matter.

Focus on the important, not just the urgent: It is easy to get caught up in the urgency of day-to-day tasks and emergencies, but it is important to remember that the most important things in life are often not urgent. By taking the time to focus on our long-term goals and values, we can ensure that we are not neglecting the things that truly matter in the long run.

Manage time effectively: Time is a finite resource, and it is important to use it wisely. This involves creating a clear sense of priorities, learning to say no to distractions and unnecessary activities, and managing our time effectively to ensure that we are making the most of every moment.

Change our perceptions to create change: In order to make meaningful changes in our lives, we must first change our perceptions and mindset. By shifting our perspective and beliefs, we can open ourselves up to new possibilities and opportunities for growth and change.

Create a compelling vision for our lives: Having a clear vision for the future is crucial to making the most of the present. By creating a compelling vision for our lives, we can ensure that our actions and decisions are aligned with our ultimate goals and values.

Live with integrity and congruence: Living a life of integrity and congruence involves aligning our actions with our values and being true to ourselves. By living in a way that is congruent with our beliefs and values, we can achieve a sense of inner peace and satisfaction that cannot be obtained through external achievements alone.

Learn to balance our roles and responsibilities: Balancing our various roles and responsibilities can be a challenging task, but it is essential to living a fulfilling and well-rounded life. By learning to prioritize our roles and responsibilities and finding a healthy balance between them, we can ensure that we are living a life that is both meaningful and fulfilling.

Summary

"First Things First" by Stephen Covey, A. Roger Merrill, and Rebecca R. Merrill is a self-help book that emphasizes the importance of prioritizing what truly matters in life. The authors argue that too often, people focus on urgent tasks and emergencies at the expense of the things that truly matter in the long run. To live a fulfilling and meaningful life, it is important to identify our core values and align our activities with those values.

The book offers a number of practical strategies for managing time, including creating a clear sense of priorities, learning to say no to distractions and unnecessary activities, and managing our time effectively to ensure that we are making the most of every moment. The authors also emphasize the importance of having a clear vision for the future, and aligning our actions and decisions with that vision.

Other key themes in the book include the importance of living with integrity and congruence, balancing our various roles and responsibilities, and learning to change our perceptions in order to create meaningful change in our lives. Overall, "First Things First" is a powerful guide for anyone who wants to live a life of purpose, meaning, and fulfillment.

CHAPTER 5

Customer Acquisition

21. The Ultimate Sales Machine by Chet Holmes

Quotes

"Sales is a process, not an event. It's something you do every day, not just when you need more business."

"Focus on the highest and best use of your time, and delegate everything else. This will free up your time to focus on what really matters."

"The most successful salespeople are those who can create a sense of urgency in their prospects."

"The best salespeople are those who are able to create and maintain relationships with their clients. This requires constant communication and follow-up."

"The key to successful selling is to identify the needs and wants of your clients, and then provide them with solutions that meet those needs and wants."

"If you want to succeed in sales, you need to have a system in place that allows you to consistently generate leads and convert them into sales."

"The best salespeople are those who are constantly learning and improving their skills. They never stop striving for excellence."

"Sales is not about selling products or services; it's about solving problems for your clients."

"If you want to succeed in sales, you need to be persistent and tenacious. You can't give up at the first sign of resistance."

"The most successful salespeople are those who are able to effectively communicate the value of their products or services to their clients."

Lessons

The importance of focus: To be successful in sales, it's crucial to focus on the highest and best use of your time. This means identifying the most important tasks that will help you achieve your goals and delegating everything else. By doing this, you'll be able to free up your time and energy to focus on what really matters.

The power of systems: Successful salespeople have a system in place that allows them to consistently generate leads and convert them into sales. By having a well-defined system, you can increase your efficiency and effectiveness, and ensure that you're not missing out on potential opportunities.

The value of relationships: Building and maintaining strong relationships with your clients is essential for long-term success in sales. This requires constant communication, follow-up, and a genuine interest in your clients' needs and wants.

The importance of persistence: Sales is not an easy job, and it requires a lot of persistence and tenacity. You need to be able to handle rejection and keep pushing forward, even when things get tough.

The need for continuous learning: To stay ahead of the competition, you need to be constantly learning and improving your skills. This means investing time and effort into learning about your industry, your clients, and the latest sales techniques and strategies.

The value of creating urgency: Creating a sense of urgency in your prospects is key to closing more sales. By highlighting the benefits of your product or service and the consequences of not taking action, you can motivate your prospects to take action now, rather than later.

Overall, The Ultimate Sales Machine provides valuable insights and practical strategies for anyone looking to improve their sales skills and achieve greater success in their career.

Summary

The Ultimate Sales Machine by Chet Holmes is a comprehensive guide to mastering the art of sales. The book provides practical strategies and techniques for building a successful sales career, including the importance of focus, systems, and relationships.

Holmes emphasizes the importance of having a well-defined system for generating leads and converting them into sales, and provides a step-by-step process for creating an effective sales funnel. He also stresses the value of focusing on the highest and best use of your time, and delegating tasks that can be handled by others.

In addition to practical sales techniques, the book also covers the importance of building and maintaining strong relationships with your clients. Holmes provides advice on how to communicate effectively with clients, and how to handle objections and close more sales.

The book also emphasizes the need for continuous learning and improvement, and provides insights into the latest sales techniques and strategies. Holmes encourages readers to invest time and effort into learning about their industry, their clients, and their competition, in order to stay ahead of the curve.

Overall, The Ultimate Sales Machine is a must-read for anyone looking to improve their sales skills and achieve greater success in their career. It provides a wealth of practical advice and strategies that can be applied by both new and experienced sales professionals.

22. Influence: The Psychology of Persuasion by Robert B. Cialdini

Quotes

"Reciprocity is a tremendous force in human life and society. It provides the means by which we enlist the cooperation of others, and it is the glue that binds together our social and cultural systems."

"The principle of scarcity is simple but powerful: the less available something is, the more valuable it is perceived to be."

"Authority can be a double-edged sword: it can be a powerful tool for influencing others, but it can also be a source of abuse and manipulation."

"Social proof is the principle that we often look to others to determine what we should do or how we should behave. It is a powerful force that can influence our decisions and actions without us even realizing it."

"Liking is a key element in the process of persuasion. People are more likely to be influenced by those they like, and they are more likely to like someone who compliments them, is similar to them, or cooperates with them."

"Commitment and consistency are powerful motivators of behavior. Once people have made a commitment, they are more likely to follow through with it, even if circumstances change."

"The principle of authority is often used in advertising and marketing to promote products and services. By associating a product with an authority figure or expert, companies can increase its perceived value and credibility."

"The principle of scarcity is particularly effective when it is combined with other principles, such as social proof or authority. When people see that others are interested in a scarce item, or that an authority figure recommends it, they are more likely to want it themselves."

"The principle of liking is particularly important in situations where people are trying to persuade others to change their beliefs or behaviors. By establishing a friendly and cooperative relationship, persuaders can increase their chances of success."

"The principle of social proof can be particularly powerful in situations where people are uncertain about what to do or how to behave. By showing that others have already made a particular choice or taken a particular action, persuaders can increase the likelihood that others will do the same."

Lessons

Understanding the principles of influence can help you become a more effective communicator: The book identifies six principles of influence -

reciprocity, commitment and consistency, social proof, liking, authority, and scarcity. Understanding these principles and applying them appropriately can help you become a more effective communicator and influence others more successfully.

People are more likely to say "yes" to those they like: Building rapport and finding commonalities with someone can increase the likelihood of them saying "yes." This can be achieved by showing genuine interest in the person, listening actively, and finding common ground.

Small commitments can lead to larger ones: Getting people to make a small commitment can increase the likelihood of them making a larger commitment later. This can be achieved by starting with small requests and gradually increasing the size of the request.

Social proof can be a powerful motivator: People are influenced by what others do and think. Therefore, showing that other people are taking a certain action or holding a certain belief can increase the likelihood of others doing the same. This can be achieved by highlighting the popularity of a product or service, or by using testimonials from satisfied customers.

Scarcity can increase the perceived value of something: People value things that are rare or in limited supply. Therefore, highlighting the scarcity of something can increase the perceived value and desirability of that thing. This can be achieved by emphasizing that a product or service is in limited supply or available for a limited time.

Authority can increase credibility and influence: People tend to comply with those they perceive as authority figures or experts. Therefore, establishing oneself as an authority or using the opinions of experts can increase the likelihood of others saying "yes." This can be achieved by highlighting one's credentials or expertise, or by using endorsements from respected authorities or experts in the field.

Summary

Influence: The Psychology of Persuasion by Robert B. Cialdini is a classic book on the topic of influence and persuasion. The book examines the psychology behind why people say "yes" and provides practical insights on how to increase one's ability to influence others.

The book is organized into six key principles of influence, which are:

Reciprocity: People feel obligated to give back to those who have given to them. Therefore, giving something to someone can increase the likelihood of them saying "yes" to a request later.

Commitment and Consistency: People tend to stick to their commitments and remain consistent with their past actions and beliefs. Therefore, getting people to make a small commitment can increase the likelihood of them making a larger commitment later.

Social Proof: People are influenced by what others do and think. Therefore, showing that other people are taking a certain action or holding a certain belief can increase the likelihood of others doing the same.

Liking: People are more likely to say "yes" to someone they like or perceive as similar to themselves. Therefore, building rapport and finding commonalities with someone can increase the likelihood of them saying "yes."

Authority: People tend to comply with those who they perceive as authority figures or experts. Therefore, establishing oneself as an authority or using the opinions of experts can increase the likelihood of others saying "yes."

Scarcity: People value things that are rare or in limited supply. Therefore, highlighting the scarcity of something can increase the perceived value and desirability of that thing.

Throughout the book, Cialdini provides numerous real-world examples and studies to illustrate each principle and provide insights into how they can be applied in various situations. The book is a valuable resource for anyone who wants to increase their ability to influence and persuade others.

23. To Sell Is Human by Daniel H. Pink

Quotes

"We're all in sales now. Each day offers a panoply of persuasions, an array of pitches, countless come-ons. We're all in non-sales selling."

"One of the most effective ways to move others is to uncover challenges they may not know they have."

"To sell well is to convince someone else to part with resources—not to deprive that person, but to leave him better off in the end."

"To be a good seller, you need empathy, buoyancy, and clarity—the capacity to recognize others' perspectives, to stay afloat in the face of rejection, and to communicate in a way that is both memorable and persuasive."

"In the age of information asymmetry, buyer beware has been replaced by seller beware. Transparency rules, and trust is the coin of the realm."

"In selling, a certain degree of improvisation is essential. Those who are most effective at it are able to think on their feet, maintain their composure, and remain flexible in the face of changing circumstances."

"Attunement—taking another's perspective—is the first step in moving others."

"In a world of instant gratification and quick fixes, selling well requires the discipline to move beyond the transaction and cultivate long-term relationships."

"Sales is no longer about creating a product that is functional or even beautiful, but about creating experiences that are memorable and shareable."

"When it comes to persuasion, nothing beats the power of serving others—of meeting their needs, solving their problems, and making their lives better."

Lessons

We're all in sales: The book argues that we are all in sales, whether we are trying to persuade others to buy a product, support an idea, or simply get along with others. Understanding the principles of selling can be useful in all aspects of our lives.

Attunement is key: The book emphasizes the importance of attunement, which means taking the perspective of others and understanding their needs, wants, and motivations. By attuning to others, we can better understand their perspective and communicate more effectively.

Problem-solving: Effective selling is not just about pushing products or services, but about solving problems and meeting the needs of customers. By understanding the challenges and goals of our customers, we can provide solutions that meet their needs.

Clarity and simplicity: To be an effective seller, it's important to communicate clearly and simply. This means focusing on the most important benefits of our products or services, and avoiding jargon or complexity that can confuse customers.

Resilience and persistence: Selling can be a challenging and often rejection-filled process. To succeed, it's important to be resilient and persistent, maintaining a positive attitude and staying motivated even when facing setbacks.

Creating experiences: In today's world, selling is not just about creating functional or attractive products, but about creating experiences that are memorable and shareable. This means focusing on the emotional benefits of our products or services, and creating experiences that customers will want to share with others.

Building relationships: Finally, effective selling is about building relationships with customers and maintaining long-term connections. This means focusing not just on the immediate sale, but on the needs and goals of our customers over the long-term.

Summary

To Sell Is Human by Daniel H. Pink is a book that explores the idea that we are all in sales, whether we are trying to sell a product, service, or simply persuade others to our point of view. The book argues that selling is a fundamental human activity that requires empathy, problem-solving, and the ability to communicate clearly and persuasively.

The book provides a number of practical tools and strategies for selling, including the importance of attunement (taking the perspective of others), the power of problem-solving, and the need for clarity and simplicity in communication. The book also emphasizes the importance of resilience and persistence in the face of rejection, and the need to focus on building relationships with customers over the long-term.

In addition to exploring these practical strategies for selling, the book also examines the changing nature of selling in the digital age, where transparency and trust are increasingly important. The book argues that effective selling in today's world is not just about creating functional or attractive products, but about creating experiences that are memorable and shareable.

Overall, To Sell Is Human is a practical and insightful guide to the art of selling, offering valuable lessons for anyone who wants to improve their ability to persuade and influence others, whether in business or in everyday life.

24. The Challenger Sale by Brent Adamson and Matthew Dixon

Quotes

"It's not about selling a product or service anymore, it's about selling a solution to a customer's problem."

"Challengers don't just build relationships, they build insight-driven relationships."

"Challengers teach their customers something new and valuable about how to compete in their market."

"The Challenger approach is about teaching, tailoring, and taking control."

"Challengers tailor their message to the specific customer and their unique situation."

"Challengers know that customers need to be shaken out of their comfort zones to make real change."

"Challengers aren't afraid to challenge the status quo and ask tough questions."

"Challengers understand that customers buy emotionally and justify rationally."

"The Challenger Sale is not about being aggressive, it's about being assertive."

"Challengers are not just selling products, they are selling insights and ideas."

Lessons

Traditional sales techniques are becoming less effective. In today's competitive market, customers are looking for more than just a sales pitch - they want a solution to their problems.

The most successful salespeople are Challengers. Challengers are salespeople who are not afraid to challenge the customer's thinking, provide new insights, and offer unique solutions.

Successful salespeople focus on teaching their customers. They help customers understand their own business better and offer solutions that are tailored to their specific needs.

The most effective salespeople use insights to differentiate themselves. By providing valuable insights and knowledge, salespeople can build trust and establish themselves as experts in their field.

Salespeople need to be assertive, but not aggressive. Challengers are assertive in their approach, but they also know when to back off and let the customer make their own decisions.

Tailoring the message to the customer is essential. Successful salespeople know how to adapt their message to the specific needs of each customer.

Building strong relationships is important, but it's not enough. Challengers focus on building insight-driven relationships that are based on mutual respect and a shared understanding of the customer's business.

Successful salespeople understand the emotional and rational drivers of customer behavior. They know that customers buy based on emotion, but also need to justify their decisions with logic and reason.

The Challenger Sale is a team effort. Salespeople need to work closely with marketing and other departments to provide customers with a cohesive and effective message.

Continuous learning is key. The most successful salespeople are always learning, growing, and improving their skills and knowledge. They never stop looking for new insights and ideas that can help them better serve their customers.

Summary

"The Challenger Sale" by Brent Adamson and Matthew Dixon is a book that challenges traditional sales techniques and offers a new approach to sales that is more effective in today's competitive market. The authors identify five different sales profiles - the Challenger, the Relationship Builder, the Hard Worker, the Lone Wolf, and the Reactive Problem Solver - and argue that the most successful salespeople are Challengers.

Challengers are salespeople who are not afraid to challenge the customer's thinking, provide new insights, and offer unique solutions. They focus on teaching their customers and tailoring their message to the specific needs of each customer. They use insights to differentiate themselves, build insight-driven relationships, and understand the emotional and rational drivers of customer behavior

. The book provides practical advice for salespeople and sales leaders on how to adopt the Challenger approach, including how to identify and develop Challengers within an organization, how to create a Challenger sales message, and how to implement Challenger sales strategies.

Overall, "The Challenger Sale" is a must-read for anyone involved in sales, marketing, or customer service. It provides a fresh perspective on how to win customers and grow business in today's competitive market.

25. Crossing the Chasm by Geoffrey A. Moore

Quotes

"Crossing the Chasm is a high-risk transition, often fatal to the prospects of the innovator's company. But for those who do cross, it is the start of a lifetime dominating an important market segment - often to the exclusion of all others."

"The chasm is a metaphor for the gap between the early adopters and the early majority."

"To cross the chasm, the marketing strategy must focus on the needs of the pragmatist customer."

"A niche market is defined as a market segment that is small enough to be neglected by large companies but profitable enough to be of interest to small companies."

"The key to succeeding in the technology market is to identify and focus on a specific market segment that has a pressing need for your technology."

"The challenge for any innovator is to cross the chasm that separates the early adopters from the early majority."

"The early majority is looking for solutions to practical problems, not for revolutionary ideas."

"To succeed in crossing the chasm, you need to understand the mindset of the early majority and create a marketing strategy that addresses their concerns."

"The chasm represents the difference between the early adopters, who are willing to take a risk on new technologies, and the early majority, who are more conservative and require more proof before making a purchasing decision."

"Crossing the chasm requires a different approach to marketing than that used in the early stages of technology adoption."

Lessons

Identify and focus on a target market: To successfully bring a product to market, it's essential to identify and focus on a specific target market. This market should be a group of customers who have similar needs, preferences, and behaviors. By focusing on a specific market, companies can tailor their products and marketing efforts to meet the unique needs of that group.

Understand the differences between early adopters and mainstream customers: Early adopters and mainstream customers have different needs, preferences, and behaviors. Understanding these differences is crucial when trying to transition from one group to the other. Companies must carefully consider these differences and develop a plan to address them.

Create a niche market: To cross the chasm, companies must establish themselves as leaders in a specific niche market. By doing so, they can gain the momentum they need to break into the mainstream market. To create a niche market, companies should focus on solving a specific problem or meeting a specific need for a particular group of customers.

Develop a well-executed plan: A grand vision is not enough to bring a product to market. Companies must develop a well-executed plan to turn that vision into a reality. This plan should include a clear understanding of the target market, the product's unique value proposition, and a marketing strategy to reach that market.

Embrace risk-taking and innovation: Successful companies are often those that are willing to take risks and try new things. To innovate, companies must be willing to take calculated risks, experiment with new ideas, and learn from failures. By doing so, they can create breakthrough products and services that meet the needs of their target market.

Summary

"Crossing the Chasm" by Geoffrey A. Moore is a book that outlines the challenges that companies face when trying to bring new products to market. The book focuses on the transition from the early adopter market to the mainstream market, which Moore refers to as the "chasm."

Moore argues that the key to successfully crossing the chasm is to focus on creating a dominant position in a niche market. This can be accomplished by identifying a target market, understanding the differences between early adopters and mainstream customers, and developing a well-executed plan to bring a product to market.

The book emphasizes the importance of understanding customer needs and preferences and tailoring products and marketing efforts to meet those needs. Moore also stresses the importance of risk-taking and innovation in creating breakthrough products and services.

Overall, "Crossing the Chasm" provides a framework for companies to successfully bring new products to market and overcome the challenges they face in transitioning from the early adopter market to the mainstream market.

CHAPTER 6

Entrepreneurship and Business

26. The E-Myth Revisited by Michael E. Gerber

Quotes

"The E-Myth is the entrepreneurial myth: the myth that most people who start small businesses are entrepreneurs, when in fact they're technicians with an entrepreneurial seizure."

"The purpose of a business is to provide a product or service that people need and will pay for. But the purpose of a business is also to provide a structure for people to work together to achieve a common goal."

"The key to success in business is not to work harder, but to work smarter."

"If your business depends on you, you don't own a business—you have a job. And it's the worst job in the world because you're working for a lunatic!"

"Systems run a business; people run around doing stuff."

"Your business is not your life. Your business is separate from your life. It's just one part of your life."

"To grow your business, you must first understand that you are not your business. Your business is an entity separate from you, and it must be treated as such."

"The key to creating a successful business is to work on your business, not just in your business."

"The most successful businesses are those that have a system in place for everything they do."

"The secret to success in business is to build a business that works without you, so that you can work on other things."

Lessons

Work on Your Business, Not in Your Business: Gerber emphasizes the importance of building a business that can function independently of the owner. This requires working on the business rather than in it, which means developing systems and processes that allow the business to run smoothly without constant supervision.

Create Systems for Everything: According to Gerber, a successful business depends on creating systems and processes for everything from customer service to marketing. These systems enable employees to produce consistent results and ensure the business operates efficiently.

Understand Your Customers' Needs: Gerber stresses the importance of understanding your customers' needs and designing your business around meeting those needs. This means focusing on delivering value and providing exceptional customer service.

Embrace Innovation: Gerber encourages entrepreneurs to embrace innovation and continuously improve their businesses. This means being open to new ideas, experimenting with new approaches, and always looking for ways to stay ahead of the competition.

Manage Your Finances: Gerber emphasizes the importance of managing your finances and tracking your expenses. This means understanding your cash flow, keeping your overhead low, and focusing on generating consistent revenue.

Balance Work and Life: Gerber reminds entrepreneurs that their business should serve their personal goals and aspirations, rather than consuming their entire life. This means finding a balance between work and personal life, and using your business as a tool to create the life you want for yourself.

Invest in Yourself: Gerber encourages entrepreneurs to invest in themselves, both personally and professionally. This means continuing to learn and grow, seeking out mentors and coaches, and focusing on personal development.

Overall, "The E-Myth Revisited" offers valuable lessons for anyone looking to build and grow a successful business. From developing systems and processes to understanding your customers' needs and managing your finances, Gerber's insights can help entrepreneurs overcome common pitfalls and achieve long-term success.

Summary

"The E-Myth Revisited" by Michael E. Gerber is a book about entrepreneurship and small business ownership. The book focuses on the concept of the "Entrepreneurial Myth," which suggests that many small business owners are primarily technicians who start a business based on their expertise in a particular field. However, they often lack the necessary business skills to run a successful enterprise, and their business ultimately fails.

Gerber argues that entrepreneurs must learn to work on their businesses, not in them. This means developing systems and processes that allow the business to function independently of the owner. The book offers practical advice on how to create these systems, manage finances, and understand customer needs.

The book also emphasizes the importance of innovation and personal development. Gerber encourages entrepreneurs to be open to new ideas and to invest in themselves both personally and professionally.

Overall, "The E-Myth Revisited" offers valuable insights into entrepreneurship and small business ownership. The book provides a roadmap for building and growing a successful business, and it emphasizes the importance of creating systems, understanding customers, and balancing work and life.

27. The Four Steps to the Epiphany by Steve Blank

Quotes

"Customers are the only source of reality."

"There are no facts inside your building, so get outside."

"No business plan survives first contact with customers."

"A startup is a temporary organization designed to search for a repeatable and scalable business model."

"The goal of a startup is to find a business model, not to execute one."

"Customer feedback is more important than perfection."

"Sales cures all."

"Get out of the building and talk to customers."

"Customer development is a process of listening to customers, understanding their problems, and validating that you've come up with a solution that solves their problems."

"Startups don't starve, they drown. They don't run out of money, they run out of time."

Lessons

Customer discovery is crucial: Blank stresses the importance of engaging with potential customers to validate assumptions and gather feedback before launching a product. This helps entrepreneurs build products that are more likely to succeed and meet the needs of their target market.

Iterate quickly: According to Blank, entrepreneurs who are able to learn and iterate quickly have a better chance of success than those who don't. This means being open to feedback, testing assumptions, and making changes as needed to stay ahead of the competition.

Focus on customer needs: Blank emphasizes the importance of focusing on customer needs and pain points when developing a product or service. By starting with the customer and working backward, entrepreneurs can build products that are more likely to be successful and meet the needs of their target audience.

Business models should be repeatable and scalable: Blank stresses the importance of finding a business model that can be replicated and scaled over time. This is the key to building a successful startup that can grow and thrive.

Failure is part of the process: Blank recognizes that failure is part of the entrepreneurial journey. He encourages entrepreneurs to embrace failure as an opportunity to learn and iterate, rather than seeing it as a setback.

Get outside the building: Blank emphasizes the importance of getting outside the building to validate assumptions and gather feedback from potential customers. This helps entrepreneurs gain valuable insights that can inform their product development and marketing strategies.

Avoid premature scaling: Blank warns against premature scaling, which can be a trap for many startups. He suggests that entrepreneurs should focus on finding a repeatable and scalable business model before scaling their operations too quickly.

Summary

"The Four Steps to the Epiphany" by Steve Blank is a book that provides a practical guide to building a successful startup. The book introduces the concept of customer development, which is a process of understanding customer needs and preferences before developing a product or service. Blank argues that this process is crucial for building a successful startup and emphasizes the importance of getting outside the building to validate assumptions and gather feedback from potential customers.

The book outlines a four-step process for customer development, which includes customer discovery, customer validation, customer creation, and company building. Each step involves different activities and strategies, such as engaging with potential customers, testing assumptions, and iterating quickly.

Blank also emphasizes the importance of finding a repeatable and scalable business model, which is the key to building a successful startup that can grow and thrive over time. He provides guidance on how to identify a business model that works and how to avoid premature scaling, which can be a trap for many startups.

Overall, "The Four Steps to the Epiphany" is a practical and insightful guide for anyone looking to build a successful startup. It provides a roadmap for customer development and emphasizes the importance of focusing on customer needs and iterating quickly to stay ahead of the competition.

28. Business Model Generation by Alexander Osterwalder and Yves Pigneur

Quotes

"A great business model can help you focus your business, define your target market and product, and ultimately help you grow and succeed."

"Business models are like recipes for creating successful businesses."

"Innovative business models can disrupt entire industries and create new ones."

"Successful companies don't just have a great product, they have a great business model that allows them to monetize their product."

"The key to a successful business model is finding a way to deliver more value to customers than your competitors, at a cost that allows you to make a profit."

"The business model canvas is a powerful tool for visualizing and analyzing your business model."

"Every business model has its own unique set of risks and opportunities.

Understanding these risks and opportunities is critical to the success of your business."

"A business model is never set in stone. It should be constantly evaluated and refined as market conditions and customer needs change."

"In the end, a business model is only as good as its execution. A great idea can only become a great business if it is executed well."

Lessons

Importance of understanding and designing a solid business model: A successful business model is a key component to the success of any company. It is important to understand the key elements that make up a successful business model and how to design one that is tailored to your specific business needs.

The value proposition is critical: A strong value proposition is at the heart of any successful business model. It is important to understand your customers' needs and what value your product or service can provide to them.

The business model canvas is a valuable tool: The business model canvas is a powerful tool for designing, analyzing, and refining your business model. It provides a clear and visual representation of your business and helps you identify areas for improvement.

The importance of testing and iterating: Business models are not set in stone and should be constantly evaluated and refined as market conditions and customer needs change. Testing and iterating on your business model can help you stay ahead of the competition and ensure long-term success.

Collaboration and teamwork are essential: Creating a successful business model requires collaboration and teamwork. It is important to involve key stakeholders and team members in the design and implementation process to ensure that everyone is on the same page and working towards a common goal.

Innovation can disrupt entire industries: Innovative business models can disrupt entire industries and create new ones. It is important to keep an eye on emerging trends and technologies and be willing to adapt and evolve your business model to stay ahead of the competition.

The importance of execution: A great idea is only the beginning. Execution is critical to the success of any business model. It is important to have a clear plan for execution and to be willing to make adjustments as needed to ensure success.

Summary

"Business Model Generation" by Alexander Osterwalder and Yves Pigneur is a guidebook for creating and refining business models. The book introduces the Business Model Canvas, a visual tool that allows entrepreneurs and business owners to analyze and design their business models. The canvas is divided into nine building blocks that represent key aspects of a business model, including customer segments, value propositions, channels, revenue streams, and key activities.

The authors discuss the importance of understanding and designing a solid business model, as well as the critical role of the value proposition. They also emphasize the importance of testing and iterating on a business model, collaboration and teamwork, and execution. The book also provides case studies of successful companies and their business models, including Apple, Google, and Amazon.

Overall, "Business Model Generation" is a practical guide for entrepreneurs, business owners, and anyone interested in designing or improving a business model. It provides a clear framework for analyzing and refining a business model, and emphasizes the importance of staying ahead of the competition through innovation and adaptation.

29. The Innovator's Dilemma by Clayton M. Christensen

Quotes

"Disruptive technologies bring to a market a very different value proposition than had been available previously. Generally, disruptive technologies underperform established products in mainstream markets. But they have other features that a few fringe (and generally new) customers value."

"An innovation that is disruptive allows a whole new population of consumers at the bottom of a market access to a product or service that was historically only accessible to consumers with a lot of money or a lot of skill."

"The reason why it is so difficult for existing firms to capitalize on disruptive innovations is that their processes and their business model that make them good at the existing business actually make them bad at competing for the disruption."

"Successful companies are usually excellent at serving their existing customers and less excellent at inventing new products or serving new customers."

"The same analytical tools that help companies manage their core businesses also work well in the search for sustaining innovations. But they are almost worthless when it comes to disruptive innovations, because those require a completely different way of thinking."

"Managers are taught to make decisions based on the data and facts that are presented to them. But sometimes the data doesn't tell the whole story, and intuition and judgment have to be used."

"Most disruptive ideas sound crazy, stupid and uneconomic at the outset; so they are often not pursued by established companies."

"Disruptive technologies typically enable new entrants to attack incumbents' least-profitable and most-overserved customers first. And then they move upmarket, taking on the incumbents' more-profitable and usually better-served customers."

"Disruptive innovation creates new markets or new ways of doing business, often by discovering new customers or new customer needs."

"The response of the successful companies that are faced with disruptive technologies is problematical. Because disruptive technologies are usually cheaper, simpler, smaller, and frequently more convenient to use, they initially present a less demanding set of performance attributes, and so they generally are not attractive to the mainstream customers and mainstream firms."

Lessons

Disruptive innovation can often come from unexpected sources: Christensen argues that disruptive innovation typically comes from smaller, less established companies that are able to create products or services that are cheaper, simpler, and more accessible than those offered by incumbents.

Established companies can struggle to adapt to disruptive innovation: Because established companies are often focused on serving their existing customers and optimizing their existing business models, they can struggle to adapt to new technologies or new customer needs that disrupt their core business.

Companies should invest in disruptive innovation: Christensen argues that established companies should create separate business units or teams that are focused on exploring new technologies and developing disruptive innovations. By doing so, companies can avoid being disrupted by new competitors.

Leaders should be willing to take risks: In order to succeed with disruptive innovation, leaders must be willing to take risks and pursue new ideas that may not initially seem profitable or attractive.

Companies should focus on customer needs: One of the keys to successful disruptive innovation is understanding the needs of customers who are currently underserved by existing products or services. By focusing on these needs, companies can create new markets and grow their business.

Summary

The Innovator's Dilemma by Clayton M. Christensen is a seminal work that explores why established companies often struggle to adapt to disruptive technologies and innovations. Christensen argues that disruptive innovations often come from smaller, less established companies that are able to create products or services that are cheaper, simpler, and more accessible than those offered by incumbents. Established companies, he argues, are often focused on serving their existing customers and optimizing their existing business models, which can make it difficult for them to adapt to new technologies or new customer needs that disrupt their core business.

To succeed with disruptive innovation, Christensen suggests that companies should invest in separate business units or teams that are focused on exploring new technologies and developing disruptive innovations. Leaders must be willing to take risks and pursue new ideas that may not initially seem profitable or attractive. Companies should also focus on understanding the needs of customers who are currently underserved by existing products or services, which can enable them to create new markets and grow their business.

Overall, The Innovator's Dilemma offers a compelling framework for understanding why established companies often struggle to innovate and adapt to new technologies and market conditions. By understanding the challenges of disruptive innovation, leaders can better position their companies for long-term success.

30. The Hard Thing About Hard Things by Ben Horowitz

Quotes

"There are no shortcuts to building a great company. Culture is the foundation of a company, and it is not set by the CEO, but by the founders. When you're building a company, it's important to remember that you're not just creating a product or a service, you're creating a culture. And that culture will determine the success or failure of your company."

"In business, it's not about being right, it's about being effective. It's not about having all the answers, it's about asking the right questions. The best CEOs are not the ones who have all the answers, but the ones who are willing to ask the tough questions and make the tough decisions."

"The hard thing isn't setting a big, hairy, audacious goal. The hard thing is laying people off when you miss the big goal. The hard thing isn't hiring great people. The hard thing is when those great people develop a sense of entitlement and start demanding unreasonable things. The hard thing isn't setting up an organizational chart. The hard thing is getting people to communicate within the organization that you just designed."

"If you don't like the hard things, then being a CEO is not the job for you. The hard things are what make the job rewarding. The hard things are what give you a sense of accomplishment. The hard things are what make it possible to build a great company."

"The most important thing that a CEO does is build a strong and cohesive team. The team is everything. A great team can accomplish anything. A mediocre team will struggle to accomplish even the simplest things."

"Great CEOs are not born, they're made. They're made by the hard things that they do. They're made by the tough decisions that they make. They're made by the challenges that they face and overcome. Being a CEO is not a job for the faint of heart. It's a job for the brave, the courageous, and the determined."

"When things get tough, you find out what you're really made of. You find out what your team is really made of. And that's when the magic happens. That's when you can accomplish things that you never thought were possible."

"The key to success is not avoiding failure, but learning from failure. Failure is inevitable in business. You will make mistakes. You will fail. The key is to learn from your mistakes and failures, and use that knowledge to improve your business."

"In a startup, the CEO is the most important person. They set the tone for the entire company. They define the culture. They make the tough decisions. They inspire the team. And they have to do all of this with very little resources, very little time, and very little money."

"The best CEOs are the ones who are constantly learning. They're constantly looking for ways to improve themselves and their businesses. They're never satisfied with the status quo. They're always pushing themselves and their teams to be better."

Lessons

Building a great company is hard work, and there are no shortcuts to success. It takes a strong culture, effective leadership, and a cohesive team to achieve great things.

CEOs should focus on being effective rather than being right. Asking the right questions, making tough decisions, and building a strong team are key to success.

The hard things are what make being a CEO rewarding. It's important to be able to handle difficult situations, such as layoffs, entitled employees, and communication issues within the organization.

A strong and cohesive team is the most important aspect of a successful company. The CEO's job is to build and lead this team.

Great CEOs are made, not born. They are made through the tough decisions they make, the challenges they face, and the hard work they put in.

Failure is inevitable in business, but it's important to learn from it and use that knowledge to improve the company

The CEO sets the tone for the entire company and defines the culture. They must be constantly learning and looking for ways to improve themselves and the business.

Being a CEO is not a job for the faint of heart. It requires bravery, determination, and the ability to handle tough situations.

Summary

"The Hard Thing About Hard Things" by Ben Horowitz is a book about the challenges of building and leading a successful company. Horowitz shares his experiences as a CEO and provides insights and lessons learned from his career in the tech industry. The book covers topics such as creating a strong culture, building a cohesive team, making tough decisions, handling failure, and constantly learning and improving. Horowitz emphasizes that being a CEO is not an easy job, but it can be rewarding if approached with determination, bravery, and the ability to handle difficult situations. Overall, the book is a valuable resource for entrepreneurs and business leaders looking to build and lead successful companies in a rapidly changing and challenging business environment.

CHAPTER 7

Finance and Wealth Building

31. Rich Dad Poor Dad by Robert T. Kiyosaki

Quotes

"The poor and the middle class work for money. The rich have money work for them."

"The single most powerful asset we all have is our mind. If it is trained well, it can create enormous wealth in what seems to be an instant."

"Financial struggle is often the result of people working all their lives for someone else."

"The rich focus on their asset columns while everyone else focuses on their income statements."

"The most important thing to remember is that you are ultimately responsible for your own financial well-being and future."

"An asset puts money in your pocket. A liability takes money out of your pocket."

"Investing in yourself is the best investment you will ever make. It will not only improve your life, it will improve the lives of all those around you."

"Money is not the most important thing in the world. Love is. Fortunately, I love money."

"The fear of losing money is real, but the fear of losing the opportunity to make money is even more real."

"The key to financial freedom and great wealth is a person's ability or skill to convert earned income into passive income and/or portfolio income."

Lessons

The difference between assets and liabilities: Kiyosaki emphasizes the importance of understanding the difference between assets and liabilities. Assets are things that put money in your pocket, while liabilities are things that take money out of your pocket. In order to become financially independent, Kiyosaki advises focusing on acquiring assets that generate passive income.

The power of financial education: Kiyosaki believes that financial education is key to achieving financial independence. He encourages readers to educate themselves about money and investing, and to learn from the successes and failures of others.

The importance of taking calculated risks: Kiyosaki argues that taking calculated risks is an essential part of building wealth. He advises readers to be willing to take risks in order to achieve their financial goals, but to also do their due diligence and minimize their potential losses.

The value of entrepreneurship: Kiyosaki is a strong proponent of entrepreneurship as a path to financial independence. He believes that starting and running your own business can be a powerful way to create wealth and control your own financial destiny.

The danger of relying on a single source of income: Kiyosaki argues that relying solely on a job for income is a risky strategy, as it puts you at the mercy of your employer and the broader economy. He advises readers to diversify their income streams and build multiple sources of income.

The importance of taking action: Kiyosaki believes that taking action is critical to achieving financial success. He encourages readers to overcome their fear and self-doubt, and to take consistent, focused action towards their financial goals.

Overall, Rich Dad Poor Dad provides a powerful framework for understanding how to build wealth and achieve financial independence. By focusing on assets, financial education, entrepreneurship, risk-taking, income diversification, and action, readers can learn how to take control of their financial future and achieve their goals.

Summary

Rich Dad Poor Dad is a personal finance book written by Robert T. Kiyosaki. The book contrasts the financial mindset and habits of Kiyosaki's two "dads": his biological father, who was a highly educated but financially struggling employee, and his best friend's father, who was a self-made millionaire and entrepreneur.

The book is divided into ten chapters, each focusing on a different lesson related to wealth-building and financial independence. Kiyosaki covers topics such as the difference between assets and liabilities, the power of financial education, the importance of taking calculated risks, and the value of entrepreneurship.

Throughout the book, Kiyosaki emphasizes the importance of mindset and the power of taking action to achieve financial success. He argues that becoming financially independent requires a shift in mindset from an employee mentality to an investor mentality, and encourages readers to focus on acquiring assets that generate passive income.

Rich Dad Poor Dad has become a classic in the personal finance genre, with its simple yet powerful lessons and relatable anecdotes. The book has inspired many readers to take control of their financial future and pursue their dreams of financial independence.

32. The Millionaire Next Door by Thomas J. Stanley and William D. Danko

Quotes

"The foundation stone of wealth accumulation is defense, and this defense should be anchored by budgeting and planning."

"Income is not wealth. Wealth is what you accumulate, not what you spend."

"If you want to be rich, you need to be financially literate."

"The very rich are those who have enough money to live on for the rest of their lives, even if they never work again." -

"Many people who live in expensive homes and drive luxury cars do not actually have much wealth. Then, we discovered something even odder: Many people who have a great deal of wealth do not even live in upscale neighborhoods."

"If you want to become wealthy, you must understand one key concept: spending less than you earn is the path to wealth."

"The most successful people in any field are those who devote the most hours to what the researchers call 'deliberate practice.'"

"The majority of millionaires are self-made. And they don't get there by doing what everyone else does."

"Wealth is not the same as income. If you make a good income each year and spend it all, you are not getting wealthier. You are just living high. Wealth is what you accumulate, not what you spend."

"The people who succeed in any venture are the people who go out and look for the circumstances they want, and if they can't find them, they create them."

Lessons

The majority of millionaires are self-made: According to the book, the majority of millionaires are self-made and did not inherit their wealth. They accumulated their wealth through hard work, frugality, and smart investments.

Live below your means: The authors emphasize the importance of living below your means if you want to accumulate wealth. This means spending less than you earn, avoiding debt, and saving and investing wisely.

Wealth is not the same as income: The book makes it clear that having a high income does not necessarily make you wealthy. Wealth is determined by what you accumulate, not what you earn. Therefore, it's important to focus on building wealth rather than just earning a high income.

Financial literacy is essential: The authors stress the importance of financial literacy for building wealth. This includes understanding the basics of personal finance, investing, and budgeting.

Hard work and deliberate practice lead to success: The book emphasizes that the most successful people in any field are those who devote the most hours to deliberate practice. This means working hard, setting goals, and constantly improving your skills and knowledge.

Avoid status spending: The authors caution against spending money on status symbols like expensive cars, clothes, and homes. Instead, they recommend investing in assets that appreciate in value over time.

Invest wisely: The book stresses the importance of investing wisely in order to build wealth over the long term. This includes diversifying your investments, avoiding high-risk investments, and taking a long-term view.

Overall, The Millionaire Next Door offers valuable insights into the habits and behaviors of wealthy people and provides practical advice on how to build wealth and achieve financial independence.

Summary

The Millionaire Next Door by Thomas J. Stanley and William D. Danko is a classic book on wealth creation and accumulation. The book is based on a comprehensive study of the habits and behaviors of millionaires in the United States.

The authors begin by debunking the myth that most millionaires are born into wealth or inherit their wealth. In fact, the majority of millionaires are self-made and have accumulated their wealth through hard work, frugality, and smart investments.

The book emphasizes the importance of living below your means, avoiding debt, and saving and investing wisely. The authors also stress the importance of financial literacy, hard work, and deliberate practice in building wealth.

The book highlights the importance of avoiding status spending and investing in assets that appreciate in value over time. The authors also provide practical advice on how to invest wisely, including diversifying your investments, avoiding high-risk investments, and taking a long-term view.

Overall, The Millionaire Next Door is a valuable resource for anyone interested in building wealth and achieving financial independence. The book provides practical advice and insights into the habits and behaviors of successful millionaires, and emphasizes the importance of discipline, hard work, and smart investments in achieving financial success.

33. The Intelligent Investor by Benjamin Graham

Quotes

"The intelligent investor is a realist who sells to optimists and buys from pessimists."

"An investment operation is one which, upon thorough analysis, promises safety of principal and a satisfactory return. Operations not meeting these requirements are speculative."

"The stock market is a voting machine in the short run and a weighing machine in the long run."

"The best investment you can make is in your own abilities. Anything you can do to develop your own abilities or business is likely to be more productive."

"The investor's chief problem, and even his worst enemy, is likely to be himself."

"The true investor welcomes volatility, for it is the only source of opportunity."

"The essence of investment management is the management of risks, not the management of returns."

"To be an investor you must be a believer in a better tomorrow."

"The investor with a portfolio of sound stocks should expect their prices to fluctuate and should neither be concerned by sizable declines nor become excited by sizable advances."

"Successful investing professionals are disciplined and consistent and they think a great deal about what they do and how they do it."

Lessons

Invest in stocks with a margin of safety: Graham's approach to investing emphasizes the importance of buying stocks at a discount to their intrinsic value. This provides a margin of safety in case the stock price falls, reducing the risk of loss.

Diversify your portfolio: Graham advises investors to diversify their portfolios to reduce risk. A diversified portfolio should include stocks from different industries, sectors, and geographies.

Focus on long-term investing: Graham's approach to investing is based on a long-term perspective, rather than trying to time the market or chase short-term gains. He advises investors to have a patient approach and focus on the fundamentals of the companies they invest in.

Be a defensive investor: Graham suggests that investors who do not have the time, knowledge, or inclination to analyze stocks should follow a defensive strategy. This involves investing in established companies with strong financials and a long history of profitability.

Avoid speculative investments: Graham distinguishes between investments and speculative ventures. He advises investors to stay away from speculative investments that promise high returns but come with high risks.

Be disciplined and rational: Graham emphasizes the importance of being disciplined and rational when investing. Investors should not let their emotions drive their investment decisions but instead rely on a sound investment strategy based on research and analysis.

Continuously educate yourself: Graham believed that successful investing requires continuous learning and improvement. Investors should stay informed about market trends, economic conditions, and the performance of the companies they invest in.

Overall, The Intelligent Investor teaches investors to be patient, disciplined, and rational in their investment approach, focusing on long-term growth and stability rather than short-term gains.

Summary

The Intelligent Investor is a classic book on value investing written by Benjamin Graham, known as the father of value investing. The book emphasizes the importance of investing with a margin of safety, diversifying your portfolio, and focusing on the long term. Graham suggests that investors should focus on the intrinsic value of a stock and not be swayed by short-term market trends or emotions.

The book also introduces the concept of the defensive investor, who focuses on investing in established companies with strong financials and a long history of profitability. Graham distinguishes between investing and speculation, advising investors to stay away from speculative investments that promise high returns but come with high risks.

The book emphasizes the importance of being disciplined and rational when investing and avoiding impulsive decisions that may lead to losses. Graham also suggests that continuous learning and improvement are essential for successful investing.

Overall, The Intelligent Investor is a comprehensive guide to value investing, providing practical advice and strategies for investors to achieve long-term growth and stability in their portfolios.

34. The Simple Path to Wealth by JL Collins

Quotes

"The single most powerful factor determining your financial success is not your investment selection, your asset allocation, or your time horizon. It is your savings rate."

"The simple approach to investing requires nothing more than making periodic investments in an index fund that tracks the overall market, then staying the course."

"A bear market is where stocks go on sale."

"Financial independence is not about retirement. It's about designing the life you want to live, and then figuring out how to pay for it."

"The beauty of investing in index funds is that you don't need to be an expert in the stock market. You just need to understand that over time, the overall market tends to go up, and you'll benefit from that growth."

"To succeed as an investor, you need to be patient, disciplined, and willing to ignore the noise of the market."

"The key to building wealth is not how much you earn, but how much you save."

"Index funds are the perfect investment vehicle for the majority of people. They are low-cost, diversified, and easy to understand."

"The biggest mistake most investors make is trying to beat the market instead of simply investing in it."

"Investing is a long-term game, and the most successful investors are those who stay the course and remain disciplined in their approach."

Lessons

The importance of saving: Collins emphasizes that saving is the single most important factor in achieving financial independence. He encourages readers to focus on increasing their savings rate, rather than obsessing over investment strategies.

The benefits of investing in index funds: Collins is a big proponent of investing in low-cost index funds that track the overall market. He argues that this approach is simple, effective, and can provide strong long-term returns.

The dangers of trying to time the market: Collins warns against the dangers of trying to time the stock market. He argues that it's impossible to predict short-term market movements, and that investors who try to do so are likely to underperform in the long run.

The importance of staying the course: Collins stresses the importance of staying disciplined and not making emotional decisions when it comes to investing. He encourages investors to remain committed to their strategy, even during periods of market volatility.

The role of financial independence: Collins argues that financial independence is not just about retiring early, but rather about designing a life that you enjoy and then figuring out how to pay for it. He encourages readers to think about their goals and priorities, and to use financial independence as a tool to achieve them.

The power of simplicity: Collins believes that investing doesn't have to be complicated, and that in fact, simplicity is often the key to success. He encourages readers to focus on simple, low-cost investment strategies that are easy to understand and implement.

Overall, "The Simple Path to Wealth" provides a clear, straightforward guide to building wealth and achieving financial independence. It emphasizes the importance of saving, investing in index funds, staying the course, and living a simple, intentional life.

Summary

"The Simple Path to Wealth" by JL Collins is a guide to building wealth and achieving financial independence through a simple, straightforward approach to investing. The book emphasizes the importance of saving, investing in low-cost index funds that track the overall market, and staying disciplined and patient in the face of market volatility. Collins argues that financial independence is not just about retiring early, but rather about designing the life you want to live and then figuring out how to pay for it. He encourages readers to focus on increasing their savings rate, living intentionally, and not getting caught up in the noise and hype of the stock market. Overall, "The Simple Path to Wealth" is a clear, concise, and practical guide to achieving financial freedom through simple, low-cost investing strategies.

35. Money Master the Game by Tony Robbins

Quotes

"The single biggest threat to your financial well-being is your own brain."

"In investing, what is comfortable is rarely profitable."

"The secret to wealth is simple: Find a way to do more for others than anyone else does. Become more valuable. Do more. Give more. Be more. Serve more."

"The only way to permanently change the temperature in the room is to reset the thermostat. In the same way, the only way to change your level of financial success 'permanently' is to reset your financial thermostat. But it is your choice whether you choose to change."

"The most important investment you can make is in yourself."

"The real key to wealth is learning how to have money work hard for you, instead of you working hard for money."

"Money is a terrible master but an excellent servant."

"The goal of investing is not to beat the market; it's to reach your financial goals with the least amount of risk possible."

"Wealth is not about having a lot of money; it's about having a lot of options."

"The greatest returns you will ever earn in life are not from investments, but from investing in yourself."

Lessons

Money Master the Game is a comprehensive book written by Tony Robbins that focuses on achieving financial freedom through investing. The book is based on interviews with some of the world's most successful investors and financial experts. Here are some of the key lessons from the book:

The importance of compound interest: Compound interest can help your investments grow significantly over time. Even small differences in investment returns can lead to significant differences in the amount of money you have in retirement.

The power of diversification: Diversifying your investments across different asset classes and sectors can help reduce risk and increase your chances of success.

The value of simplicity: Investing doesn't have to be complicated. Simple, low-cost index funds can be a great way to achieve solid returns over the long term.

The role of emotions in investing: Emotions such as fear and greed can lead to poor investment decisions. It's important to have a solid investment plan and to stick to it, even during market downturns.

The importance of fees: High fees can eat into your investment returns over time. Choosing low-cost investments and minimizing fees can help you keep more of your investment gains.

The need for a financial advisor: A good financial advisor can provide valuable guidance and help you make sound investment decisions based on your goals and risk tolerance.

The importance of giving back: Money can be a powerful tool for making a positive impact in the world. Donating to charity can be a fulfilling way to use your wealth to make a difference.

Overall, Money Master the Game provides a wealth of information and practical advice for anyone looking to achieve financial freedom through investing. By following these lessons, you can increase your chances of success and enjoy a more secure financial future.

Summary

Money Master the Game by Tony Robbins is a comprehensive guide to achieving financial freedom through investing. The book is based on interviews with some of the world's most successful investors and financial experts.

The book emphasizes the importance of compound interest, diversification, simplicity, and controlling emotions when investing. It also highlights the impact of high fees on investment returns and the importance of working with a financial advisor to make sound investment decisions.

In addition, the book encourages readers to give back by donating to charity as a way to make a positive impact in the world.

CHAPTER 8

Communication and Public Speaking

36. Talk Like TED by Carmine Gallo

Quotes

"Passion is the foundation of great communication. If you're not passionate about your message, no one else will be either."

"Emotion is the key to engaging your audience. People remember how you make them feel, not what you say."

"Storytelling is the most powerful way to put ideas into the world today. Stories inspire, motivate, and connect us to one another."

"Simplicity is the ultimate sophistication. The most memorable presentations are those that are simple, clear, and focused."

"Use visuals to enhance your message, not distract from it. A well-designed slide can be worth a thousand words."

"Practice, practice, practice. The more you rehearse your presentation, the more confident and natural you'll be on stage."

"Humor is a powerful tool for engaging your audience. Laughter breaks down barriers and helps create a connection with your listeners."

"Authenticity is key. Be yourself and speak from the heart. Your audience can tell when you're being fake, so don't try to be someone you're not."

"Passion, curiosity, and a desire to make a difference are the hallmarks of great TED speakers. These qualities are what make their presentations so compelling and inspiring."

"Remember that public speaking is not about you, it's about your audience. Focus on what they need to hear, and how you can best communicate your message to them."

Lessons

One of the key lessons from "Talk Like TED" by Carmine Gallo is the importance of delivering a compelling and engaging presentation. Gallo suggests that the most successful TED speakers share three key qualities: they are emotional, novel, and memorable. Here are some specific lessons from the book:

Start with a strong opening: Gallo emphasizes the importance of starting your presentation with a hook that captures the audience's attention and draws them in.

Use storytelling: Instead of just presenting facts and data, use stories to illustrate your points and make the information more relatable and memorable.

Use visual aids: Gallo suggests using visually interesting slides or props to enhance your presentation and create a more engaging experience for your audience.

Be authentic: The best TED speakers are those who are genuine and passionate about their topic. Don't try to be someone you're not; instead, be yourself and let your passion shine through.

Practice, practice, practice: Delivering a great presentation takes time and effort. Gallo recommends practicing your talk multiple times to ensure that you're comfortable with the material and can deliver it smoothly.

Overall, the lesson from "Talk Like TED" is that delivering a great presentation is not just about conveying information, but also about engaging your audience on an emotional level and creating a memorable experience for them. By following these tips and focusing on delivering an authentic, engaging talk, you can inspire and motivate your audience to take action and make a real impact.

Summary

"Talk Like TED" by Carmine Gallo is a book about the qualities and characteristics that make TED talks so engaging and memorable. Through analysis of successful TED talks and interviews with top TED presenters,

Gallo identifies three key elements that all great TED talks share: they are emotional, novel, and memorable.

The book is divided into three sections, each focusing on one of these elements. In the emotional section, Gallo discusses the importance of connecting with your audience on an emotional level by sharing personal stories, using humor, and delivering a message that resonates with their values and beliefs. In the novel section, Gallo explores the importance of presenting new and interesting ideas, using creative visuals, and providing a fresh perspective on a familiar topic. In the memorable section, Gallo discusses the importance of delivering a message that is memorable, actionable, and leaves a lasting impression on the audience.

Throughout the book, Gallo provides numerous examples of successful TED talks and offers practical advice on how to incorporate the three elements into your own presentations. He also emphasizes the importance of practice, authenticity, and passion in delivering a great talk.

Overall, "Talk Like TED" is a valuable resource for anyone looking to improve their public speaking skills and deliver a presentation that is both engaging and impactful

37. Presentation Zen by Garr Reynolds

Quotes

"Design is not just what it looks like and feels like. Design is how it works." - Steve Jobs

"Simplicity is about subtracting the obvious and adding the meaningful." - John Maeda

"Presentation design is not about decorating ideas with pretty pictures. It's about thinking clearly and expressing ideas powerfully."

"Good design is invisible. It shouldn't draw attention to itself, but instead enhance the message and facilitate communication."

"The most effective presentations are those that focus on the audience, not the presenter. Think about what your audience needs to hear, and how you can best communicate your message to them."

"Visuals should be used to support the message, not distract from it. Use images and graphics that are simple, powerful, and meaningful."

"Less is more. The simpler your design, the more impact it will have on your audience."

"Practice, practice, practice. The more you rehearse your presentation, the more confident and effective you'll be on stage."

"Authenticity is key. Your audience wants to hear from a real person, not a scripted robot. Be yourself and speak from the heart."

"Remember that presentation design is an art, not a science. There are no hard and fast rules, but rather principles and guidelines that can be adapted and applied to each unique situation."

Lessons

Simplify your message: The most effective presentations are often the simplest. Instead of overwhelming your audience with too much information, focus on distilling your message down to its essence. This can help to make your presentation more memorable and impactful.

Use visuals: Our brains are wired to process visual information more easily than text, so incorporating relevant images or graphics can help to reinforce your message and make it more memorable. Additionally, visuals can help to break up the monotony of a text-heavy presentation and keep your audience engaged.

Tell a story: People are naturally drawn to stories, and using them in your presentations can help to capture your audience's attention and make your message more memorable. By framing your ideas within a compelling narrative, you can create a more engaging and impactful presentation.

Keep it simple: When it comes to design, less is often more. Use a simple and consistent design throughout your presentation to avoid overwhelming your audience with too much visual noise.

Practice and prepare: No matter how well-designed your presentation is, it won't be effective if you're not prepared. Take the time to practice your presentation and familiarize yourself with your materials. This can help to build your confidence and ensure that your presentation goes smoothly.

Engage with your audience: Finally, it's important to remember that presentations are not one-sided lectures. Engage with your audience by asking questions, soliciting feedback, and encouraging discussion. This can help to make your presentation more interactive and memorable, and it can also help to build a connection between you and your audience.

Summary

"Presentation Zen" by Garr Reynolds is a book that emphasizes the importance of creating simple, engaging, and impactful presentations. The book provides practical tips and strategies for designing effective presentations, including the use of visuals, storytelling, and simple design principles. Reynolds encourages presenters to focus on delivering a clear and concise message, and to engage with their audience through questions, feedback, and discussion. Additionally, the book stresses the importance of practice and preparation, as well as the need to stay relaxed and composed while giving a presentation. Overall, "Presentation Zen" is a valuable resource for anyone who wants to improve their presentation skills and create more memorable and impactful presentations.

38. Confessions of a Public Speaker by Scott Berkun

Quotes

"The best public speakers are not born, they're made. Anyone can become a great speaker with practice and dedication."

"Fear is a natural part of public speaking. The key is to use that fear to fuel your passion and drive to succeed."

"The most effective presentations are those that tell a story. People remember stories much more than they remember facts and figures."

"The secret to engaging your audience is to be yourself. Your authenticity and personality are what will make your presentation unique and memorable."

"Audiences want to be entertained, not just informed. Use humor, stories, and interactive elements to keep them engaged and interested."

"Preparation is key. The more you prepare for your presentation, the more confident and polished you'll be on stage."

"The best speakers are those who are able to connect with their audience on an emotional level. Use your body language and tone of voice to convey your message with passion and conviction."

"Don't be afraid to make mistakes. Even the best speakers stumble from time to time. The key is to keep going and not let your mistakes derail your presentation."

"Feedback is essential for growth. Seek out constructive criticism and use it to improve your skills and become a better speaker."

"Remember that public speaking is a privilege, not a chore. Embrace the opportunity to share your message with others and make a difference in the world."

Lessons

Public speaking is a skill that can be learned and improved with practice.

Effective public speaking requires preparation, including researching your topic, understanding your audience, and practicing your delivery.

Engaging your audience and connecting with them emotionally is key to delivering a successful presentation.

Humor can be a powerful tool in public speaking, but it must be used carefully and appropriately.

Public speaking is a performance, and like any performance, it requires a certain level of showmanship and stage presence.

Being authentic and genuine in your delivery can help build trust and credibility with your audience.

Embracing your mistakes and learning from them is an important part of improving your public speaking skills.

Public speaking is a form of leadership, and the ability to communicate effectively is a critical skill for anyone in a leadership role.

To become a successful public speaker, it's important to seek out opportunities to speak and to continually challenge yourself to improve.

Ultimately, the key to successful public speaking is to be passionate about your topic, to be well-prepared, and to genuinely care about your audience and their needs.

Summary

"Confessions of a Public Speaker" by Scott Berkun is a book that provides insights and advice for people who want to improve their public speaking skills. The book is based on the author's experiences as a professional speaker and offers practical tips and strategies for preparing and delivering effective presentations.

Throughout the book, Berkun emphasizes the importance of practice, preparation, and audience engagement. He discusses the role of humor in public speaking and offers advice on how to use it effectively. He also shares his thoughts on the art of storytelling and the importance of authenticity in public speaking.

In addition, the book includes anecdotes and personal stories from Berkun's own experiences as a public speaker, offering insights into the challenges and rewards of this career path. Overall, "Confessions of a Public Speaker" is an engaging and informative guide for anyone looking to improve their public speaking skills, whether for personal or professional reasons.

39. The Presentation Secrets of Steve Jobs by Carmine Gallo

Quotes

"The most powerful person in the world is the storyteller. The storyteller sets the vision, values and agenda of an entire generation."

"The key to a great presentation is to tell a story that captivates your audience and inspires them to take action."

"Simplicity is the ultimate sophistication. The simpler your message, the more memorable it will be."

"Focus on the benefits, not the features. People don't buy what you do, they buy why you do it."

"Use visuals to communicate your message. A picture is worth a thousand words, and a well-designed slide can be worth a million."

"Passion is contagious. If you're passionate about what you're presenting, your audience will be too."

"Practice, practice, practice. The more you rehearse your presentation, the more confident and polished you'll be on stage."

"Be authentic and genuine. Your audience can tell when you're being fake, so be yourself and speak from the heart."

"Use humor and emotion to connect with your audience. Laughter and tears are powerful tools for engaging your listeners."

"End with a call to action. Your presentation should inspire your audience to take action, whether it's to buy your product, join your cause, or make a change in their lives."

Lessons

The Presentation Secrets of Steve Jobs by Carmine Gallo provides several valuable lessons for anyone who wants to improve their presentation skills.

Here are some of the key takeaways:

Storytelling is key: Jobs believed that storytelling was the most powerful tool for communicating ideas and inspiring others. By crafting a compelling narrative, presenters can capture their audience's attention and make their message more memorable.

Keep it simple: Jobs was a master of simplicity, and he believed that the best presentations were those that conveyed a clear and simple message. Avoid jargon, complex language, and unnecessary details, and focus on communicating your message in a straightforward and accessible way.

Design matters: Jobs understood the importance of design in creating a great user experience, and this philosophy extended to his presentations as well. Use visuals and design elements to enhance your message and create a cohesive and polished presentation.

Rehearse, rehearse, rehearse: Jobs was known for his meticulous preparation, and he would often spend hours rehearsing his presentations. By practicing your presentation multiple times, you can build confidence, identify areas that need improvement, and ensure that you deliver a polished and engaging performance

Connect with your audience: Jobs had a powerful stage presence, and he was able to connect with his audience on a deep and emotional level. By using eye contact, gestures, and vocal inflection, you can build a connection with your audience and make your presentation more engaging and impactful.

Overall, The Presentation Secrets of Steve Jobs emphasizes the importance of preparation, simplicity, and storytelling in creating effective and memorable presentations. By following these principles, anyone can improve their presentation skills and become a more effective communicator..

Summary

The Presentation Secrets of Steve Jobs by Carmine Gallo is a book that examines the techniques and strategies used by Steve Jobs to create engaging and effective presentations. Through a series of case studies and examples, the book highlights the importance of storytelling, simplicity, design, rehearsal, and audience connection in creating powerful and memorable presentations.

The book provides a detailed analysis of Jobs' presentations, including his use of visuals, language, and gestures to create a cohesive and impactful message. It also explores the principles behind Jobs' design philosophy, which emphasized the importance of simplicity, functionality, and usability.

Throughout the book, Gallo emphasizes the importance of preparation and practice in creating great presentations, and provides practical advice on how to improve one's presentation skills. Whether you are a business leader, a student, or anyone else who wants to improve their communication skills, The Presentation Secrets of Steve Jobs is a valuable resource for anyone who wants to create effective and memorable presentations.

40.   TED Talks by Chris Anderson

Quotes

"The only way we can take someone else's perspective is if we are willing to temporarily step out of our own." - Chris Anderson

"A great talk is one that sparks imagination, creates new ways of seeing things, and leaves the listener feeling enriched." - Chris Anderson

"The most powerful talks are often the most personal. They connect with our deepest emotions and invite us to share in the speaker's experience." - Chris Anderson

"Passion is infectious. When we see someone who truly cares about something, it inspires us to care as well." - Chris Anderson

"The art of persuasion isn't about using fancy words or impressive data points. It's about connecting with your audience on an emotional level and making them care about what you have to say."

"The best way to engage an audience is to make them feel like active participants in the talk, rather than passive listeners."

"Authenticity is key to building trust with your audience. If you're not being true to yourself and your message, your listeners will be able to sense it."

"The most successful speakers are those who are able to adapt their message to fit the needs of their audience."

"The key to a great talk isn't just what you say, it's how you say it. Your tone, body language, and delivery all play a critical role in engaging your audience."

"The most memorable talks are the ones that tell a story. Stories are powerful because they help us connect with our humanity and see the world in a new light."

Lessons

Focus on your idea: The most important part of a great TED talk is the idea that you're sharing. It should be something that is important to you, something that you're passionate about, and something that has the potential to inspire and engage your audience.

Tell a story: One of the most effective ways to engage your audience is by telling a story. Stories help people connect with your message on an emotional level and can help you make your point in a more memorable way.

Keep it simple: TED talks are known for being concise and to the point. When preparing your talk, focus on simplifying your message and getting rid of anything that doesn't directly support your core idea.

Practice, practice, practice: Great TED speakers don't just show up and wing it. They put in hours of preparation and practice to make sure their talk is polished and flows seamlessly.

Be authentic: Your audience will be able to tell if you're not being genuine, so it's important to be authentic and speak from the heart. Share your personal experiences and emotions, and don't be afraid to be vulnerable.

Engage your audience: A great TED talk isn't just a monologue – it's a conversation between you and your audience. Look for ways to engage your audience throughout your talk, such as asking questions, using humor, or getting them to participate in an activity.

Use visuals effectively: Visuals can be a powerful tool for enhancing your message, but they can also be distracting if not used correctly. Make sure your visuals are clear, simple, and support your core idea.

Respect your audience's time: TED talks are typically limited to 18 minutes, and for good reason. Your audience's time is valuable, so make sure every minute of your talk is worth their attention.

Keep learning and growing: Great speakers are always looking for ways to improve and grow. Keep practicing, seeking feedback, and learning from other speakers to continue honing your skills.

Summary

In his book "TED Talks," Chris Anderson shares insights and lessons on how to deliver a powerful and memorable talk. Drawing from his experience as the curator of the TED conference, Anderson explains what makes a great talk and offers practical advice on how to prepare, deliver, and improve your public speaking skills. He emphasizes the importance of focusing on your core idea, telling a compelling story, and engaging your audience through a conversational style. Anderson also stresses the need to be authentic and vulnerable, to use visuals effectively, and to respect your audience's time by keeping your talk concise and to the point. Ultimately, "TED Talks" is a valuable resource for anyone who wants to improve their public speaking skills and deliver a memorable talk that inspires and moves their audience.

CHAPTER 9

Mindset and Attitude

41.   Mindset: The New Psychology of Success by Carol S. Dweck

Quotes

"In a growth mindset, challenges are exciting rather than threatening. So rather than thinking, oh, I'm going to reveal my weaknesses, you say, wow, here's a chance to grow."

"The passion for stretching yourself and sticking to it, even (or especially) when it's not going well, is the hallmark of the growth mindset. This is the mindset that allows people to thrive during some of the most challenging times in their lives."

"The view you adopt for yourself profoundly affects the way you lead your life."

"Why waste time proving over and over how great you are, when you could be getting better? Why hide deficiencies instead of overcoming them? Why look for friends or partners who will just shore up your self-esteem instead of ones who will also challenge you to grow? And why seek out the tried and true, instead of experiences that will stretch you? The passion for stretching yourself and sticking to it, even (or especially) when it's not going well, is the hallmark of the growth mindset."

"If parents want to give their children a gift, the best thing they can do is to teach their children to love challenges, be intrigued by mistakes, enjoy effort, and keep on learning. That way, their children don't have to be slaves of praise. They will have a lifelong way to build and repair their own confidence."

"The fixed mindset can negatively impact all aspects of your life, from relationships and parenting to work and achievement. A growth mindset, on the other hand, can contribute to success and fulfillment in all of these areas."

"Effort is one of the things that gives meaning to life. Effort means you care about something, that something is important to you, and you are willing to work for it. It would be an impoverished existence if you were not willing to value things and commit yourself to working toward them."

"In the fixed mindset, imperfections are shameful and never to be exposed. The growth mindset, on the other hand, is a little more forgiving and realistic. Mistakes can be painful, but they do not define you."

"We like to think of our champions and idols as superheroes who were born different from us. We don't like to think of them as relatively ordinary people who made themselves extraordinary."

"Becoming is better than being. The fixed mindset does not allow people the luxury of becoming. They have to already be."

"People in a growth mindset don't just seek challenge, they thrive on it. The bigger the challenge, the more they stretch."

"If you're not failing, you're not learning. And if you're not learning, you're not growing."

"The growth mindset allows people to value what they're doing regardless of the outcome."

"A growth mindset is not just about effort. Perhaps the most common misconception is simply equating the growth mindset with effort. Certainly, effort is key for students' achievement, but it's not the only thing. Students need to try new strategies and seek input from others when they're stuck. They need this repertoire of approaches—not just sheer effort—to learn and improve."

"The whole point of mindfulness is to observe and accept what's happening inside you and outside you, without judgment. It's not to fight it, but to just see it and accept it."

Lessons

The power of mindset: The book emphasizes the importance of our mindset, whether it is a fixed mindset or a growth mindset, and how it can impact our personal and professional lives.

Embrace challenges: The book teaches us that challenges are opportunities for growth and development. Embracing challenges helps us to learn new things, acquire new skills and become better versions of ourselves.

The importance of effort: The book emphasizes the role of effort in achieving success. It argues that success is not just about talent or intelligence, but also about hard work and perseverance.

The power of positive self-talk: The book highlights the importance of positive self-talk and how it can help us overcome self-doubt, build resilience and achieve our goals.

Embrace failure: The book emphasizes that failure is not a setback but an opportunity for growth. Embracing failure helps us to learn from our mistakes, improve our skills and become more successful in the long run.

Cultivate a growth mindset: The book encourages us to cultivate a growth mindset, which is a belief that we can improve and develop our abilities through hard work and dedication. A growth mindset helps us to embrace challenges, learn from failure and achieve our goals.

The importance of continuous learning: The book emphasizes the importance of continuous learning and growth. It encourages us to seek out new challenges, acquire new skills and knowledge, and to keep learning throughout our lives.

Encourage a growth mindset in others: The book argues that as parents, teachers, managers, and leaders, we can help others to cultivate a growth mindset by encouraging effort, embracing failure, and providing opportunities for growth and development.

Mindfulness: The book emphasizes the importance of mindfulness in developing a growth mindset. Mindfulness helps us to be present in the moment, observe our thoughts and emotions, and accept them without judgment.

Summary

In her book Mindset: The New Psychology of Success, Carol S. Dweck presents the concept of mindset, which refers to the beliefs and attitudes we hold about ourselves and our abilities. She argues that there are two main types of mindset: a fixed mindset and a growth mindset.

In a fixed mindset, people believe that their abilities and traits are fixed and cannot be changed. They tend to avoid challenges, give up easily, and feel threatened by the success of others. On the other hand, in a growth mindset, people believe that their abilities can be developed through hard work and dedication. They embrace challenges, persist in the face of setbacks, and are inspired by the success of others.

Dweck discusses the impact of mindset on various aspects of our lives, including relationships, parenting, education, and work. She argues that a growth mindset can lead to greater success and fulfillment in all of these areas, while a fixed mindset can hold us back.

Throughout the book, Dweck provides numerous examples and case studies to illustrate the concepts of fixed and growth mindsets. She also offers practical advice on how to develop a growth mindset and cultivate it in others.

Overall, Mindset is a thought-provoking and inspiring book that challenges readers to reevaluate their beliefs about their own abilities and encourages them to embrace challenges, learn from failure, and strive for continuous growth and development.

42. The 5 Love Languages by Gary Chapman

Quotes

"Love is a choice you make from moment to moment."

"The in-love experience does not focus on our own growth nor on the growth and development of the other person. Rather, it gives us the sense that we have arrived and that we do not need further growth."

"Love is not a feeling, Mr. Chapman. It's an attitude. A choice. And that choice is made every day."

"If I speak in the tongues of men or of angels, but do not have love, I am only a resounding gong or a clanging cymbal."

"Love is the most important ingredient of your marriage. It is the bond that holds your relationship together."

"The object of love is not getting something you want but doing something for the well-being of the one you love."

"Love is a choice you make from moment to moment, every day of your life. You cannot wait for someone else to make that choice for you."

"We all have a deep need for love and connection, and when we feel loved, it can motivate us to achieve great things."

"The words 'I love you' are important, but they are not enough. We must express our love in a way that speaks to our partner's individual love language."

"The way we give and receive love is often shaped by our childhood experiences and the models of love we observed growing up."

Lessons

One of the key lessons from The 5 Love Languages by Gary Chapman is that people have different ways of expressing and receiving love. Chapman identifies five different love languages: Words of Affirmation, Quality Time, Receiving Gifts, Acts of Service, and Physical Touch.

According to Chapman, individuals have a primary love language through which they feel most loved and valued, and it is important for partners to understand and communicate with each other in their respective love languages. When partners speak each other's love languages, they can strengthen their emotional connection, increase intimacy, and deepen their bond.

Another important lesson from the book is that love is not just a feeling, but also a choice and an action. Choosing to love someone and demonstrating that love through actions, such as acts of service or quality time, can help build and maintain strong relationships. Chapman emphasizes that expressing love in a way that speaks to your partner's individual love language is crucial for a successful relationship.

Overall, the book highlights the importance of understanding and communicating with your partner in their preferred love language, and actively choosing to show love and appreciation in meaningful ways.

Summary

The 5 Love Languages by Gary Chapman is a book that explores the different ways people express and receive love in their relationships. According to Chapman, people have different primary love languages: Words of Affirmation, Quality Time, Receiving Gifts, Acts of Service, and Physical Touch.

Chapman explains that understanding and communicating with your partner in their preferred love language is crucial for a successful relationship. When partners speak each other's love languages, they can strengthen their emotional connection, increase intimacy, and deepen their bond.

The book emphasizes that expressing love is not just a feeling, but also a choice and an action. Choosing to love someone and demonstrating that love through actions, such as acts of service or quality time, can help build and maintain strong relationships.

Overall, The 5 Love Languages provides a framework for understanding how people give and receive love, and offers practical advice on how to communicate and show love in meaningful ways. The book has been widely praised for its insights into relationship dynamics and has helped many couples improve their communication and connection.

43. The Art of Possibility by Rosamund Stone Zander and Benjamin Zander

Quotes

"The practice of possibility is about making new assumptions, seeing things differently, and exploring new avenues for action."

"Our perceptions shape our reality. By shifting our perceptions, we can change the world we live in."

"The way we talk to ourselves and others can have a powerful impact on our mindset and our ability to achieve our goals."

"Leadership is about empowering others and creating a culture of possibility. When people feel heard, seen, and valued, they are more likely to contribute their best work."

"Mistakes and failures are opportunities for growth and learning. We should embrace them, rather than fear them."

"The concept of 'scarcity' is a self-fulfilling prophecy. By focusing on abundance and possibility, we can create more of what we want in life."

"Authentic communication is key to building trust and fostering positive relationships. We need to be willing to be vulnerable and share our true selves with others."

"We can choose to live in a world of measurement and comparison, or a world of possibility and connection. The choice is ours."

"Creativity is not just for artists, but for everyone. We all have the capacity to create and innovate in our own unique way."

"The Art of Possibility is about living a life of abundance, creativity, and connection. It's about choosing to see the world through a lens of possibility, rather than limitation."

Lessons

Change your perspective: The book emphasizes the importance of shifting one's perspective and reframing situations. By doing so, you can open yourself up to new possibilities and ways of thinking.

Focus on what you can control: The authors encourage readers to focus on what they can control and to let go of what they cannot control. This involves taking responsibility for one's own life and decisions.

Embrace mistakes: The authors emphasize the importance of embracing mistakes as opportunities for learning and growth. Rather than seeing mistakes as failures, they encourage readers to view them as part of the process of achieving success.

Lead from possibility: The book encourages readers to lead from a place of possibility and abundance rather than scarcity. This involves empowering others and creating space for them to develop their own leadership skills.

Live in the present: The authors emphasize the importance of living in the present moment and enjoying the journey. This involves letting go of past regrets and future worries and embracing the present moment fully.

Be open to new experiences: The book encourages readers to be open to new experiences and to step out of their comfort zones. This involves taking risks and being willing to try new things, even if they seem daunting at first.

Overall, the book teaches readers to adopt a mindset of possibility, to focus on what they can control, and to approach life with a sense of openness and curiosity.

Summary

The Art of Possibility is a book by Rosamund Stone Zander and Benjamin Zander that offers a new perspective on life and leadership. The authors argue that by shifting our mindset and adopting a mindset of possibility, we can unlock our full potential and achieve our goals.

The book is divided into twelve chapters, each of which explores a different aspect of possibility. The authors encourage readers to embrace mistakes as opportunities for growth, to let go of past regrets and future worries, and to focus on what they can control. They also emphasize the importance of being open to new experiences, taking risks, and approaching life with a sense of curiosity and wonder.

The book provides practical tools and strategies for cultivating a mindset of possibility, such as reframing situations, embracing failure, and celebrating small victories. The authors also share inspiring stories of individuals who have overcome adversity and achieved great success by adopting a mindset of possibility.

Overall, The Art of Possibility is a thought-provoking and uplifting book that challenges readers to think differently about their lives and leadership. It provides a roadmap for unlocking our full potential and achieving our goals by embracing a mindset of possibility.

44. The Happiness Advantage by Shawn Achor

Quotes

"Happiness is not the result of success. Success is the result of happiness."

"Positive emotions fuel success. When we're happy, we're more productive, creative, and resilient."

"Our brains are designed to perform better when we're happy. We're more likely to see opportunities, solve problems, and make better decisions."

"Happiness is a choice. We can train our brains to be more positive by cultivating gratitude, mindfulness, and other positive habits."

"Social connections are essential for happiness. We need to invest in our relationships and make time for meaningful interactions with others."

"Success is not a solo endeavor. We need to build a supportive team and collaborate with others to achieve our goals."

"Resilience is key to overcoming challenges and bouncing back from setbacks. We can develop resilience by cultivating a growth mindset and learning from failures."

"Optimism is not about ignoring the negative, but rather seeing the positive in the face of adversity. We can train our brains to be more optimistic by focusing on our strengths and solutions."

"Happiness is contagious. When we're happy, we spread positive emotions to those around us, creating a ripple effect of positivity."

"Happiness is not a destination, but a journey. We need to enjoy the process and find joy in the present moment, rather than just striving for future success."

Lessons

Happiness leads to success, not the other way around. Achor argues that by prioritizing happiness and cultivating positive emotions, we can improve our cognitive abilities, creativity, and productivity, leading to greater success in all areas of life.

We can train our brains to be more positive. Achor suggests that we can build new neural pathways in our brains by intentionally focusing on positive thoughts and emotions. By engaging in simple practices like gratitude exercises and acts of kindness, we can rewire our brains for greater happiness and well-being.

Social connections are critical to happiness. Achor argues that social support is one of the most important factors in promoting happiness and resilience. By building strong relationships with friends, family, and colleagues, we can improve our emotional well-being and overcome challenges more effectively.

Mindfulness is a powerful tool for happiness. Achor suggests that by practicing mindfulness, we can become more aware of our thoughts and emotions, and better able to regulate them in positive ways. Mindfulness can help us to reduce stress, improve our mood, and increase our overall sense of well-being.

Happiness is contagious. Achor argues that our emotions are highly contagious, and that by cultivating happiness within ourselves, we can spread positive emotions to others. By bringing a positive attitude and mindset to our interactions with others, we can create a ripple effect of positivity and improve the well-being of those around us. Overall, the key lesson of "The Happiness Advantage" is that happiness is not just a byproduct of success, but a critical component of it. By prioritizing our own happiness and cultivating positive emotions, we can improve our cognitive abilities, creativity, and productivity, and achieve greater success in all areas of our lives.

Summary

"The Happiness Advantage" by Shawn Achor is a book that explores the relationship between happiness and success. Achor argues that happiness is not just a byproduct of success, but rather a critical component of it. By prioritizing happiness and cultivating positive emotions, we can improve our cognitive abilities, creativity, and productivity, leading to greater success in all areas of life.

The book outlines several strategies for cultivating happiness, including building social connections, practicing mindfulness, and focusing on positive thoughts and emotions. Achor suggests that by intentionally focusing on positive habits and behaviors, we can train our brains to be more positive and build new neural pathways that support greater happiness and well-being.

Throughout the book, Achor also emphasizes the importance of social connections in promoting happiness and resilience. He argues that by building strong relationships with friends, family, and colleagues, we can improve our emotional well-being and overcome challenges more effectively.

Overall, "The Happiness Advantage" is a powerful reminder that happiness is within our control and that cultivating a positive mindset can have a profound impact on our success and well-being. The book provides practical strategies and insights for anyone looking to increase their happiness and achieve greater success in their personal and professional lives.

45.   The Power of Now by Eckhart Tolle

Quotes

"The past has no power over the present moment."

"You cannot find yourself by going into the past. You can find yourself by coming into the present."

"To be identified with your mind is to be trapped in time: the compulsion to live almost exclusively through memory and anticipation."

"The more attention you give to the past, the more you energize it, and the more likely it is that you will re-create it."

"All negativity is caused by an accumulation of psychological time and denial of the present. Unease, anxiety, tension, stress, worry - all forms of fear - are caused by too much future, and not enough presence."

"The mind constantly seeks to deny or escape the Now by projecting itself into the future or the past."

"As soon as you honor the present moment, all unhappiness and struggle dissolve, and life begins to flow with joy and ease."

"The primary cause of unhappiness is never the situation but your thoughts about it."

"The joy of Being, which is the only true happiness, cannot come to you through any form, possession, achievement, person, or event - through anything that happens. That joy cannot come to you - ever. It emanates from the formless dimension within you, from consciousness itself and thus is one with who you are."

"All you really need to do is accept this moment fully. You are then at ease in the here and now and at ease with yourself."

Lessons

Live in the present moment: Tolle emphasizes that the present moment is all we truly have, and encourages readers to let go of the past and the future, and focus on the present moment.

The mind can be a powerful tool or a source of suffering: Tolle suggests that the mind can be either a powerful instrument for problem-solving, or a source of suffering if we allow it to control us.

Don't identify with your thoughts: Tolle teaches readers to observe their thoughts without identifying with them, recognizing that they are not who we truly are.

Acceptance and non-resistance: Tolle encourages readers to practice acceptance and non-resistance, to work with the present moment rather than struggling against it.

The interconnectedness of all things: Tolle emphasizes the interconnectedness of all things, and encourages readers to recognize their fundamental unity with all of creation.

The importance of stillness and silence: Tolle teaches readers to cultivate stillness and silence, as a way to connect with their inner being and experience a deeper sense of peace and joy.

Letting go of the ego: Tolle suggests that the ego, or the false sense of self, is the root of much of our suffering, and encourages readers to let go of it and connect with their true nature.

Overall, "The Power of Now" offers a transformative perspective on life, inviting readers to awaken to the present moment, let go of the past and future, and connect with their inner being.

Summary

The Power of Now is a spiritual guidebook that aims to help readers achieve a greater level of self-awareness and inner peace. The book is divided into ten chapters, each of which explores a different aspect of human consciousness and the obstacles that prevent us from experiencing the present moment fully.

The central thesis of the book is that most of our problems arise from our inability to live in the present moment. We are either preoccupied with regrets and memories of the past or anxious about the future, and this prevents us from fully experiencing the beauty of the present moment. Eckhart Tolle argues that the only way to achieve true happiness and fulfillment is to learn to live in the present moment and to be fully aware of our thoughts and emotions.

The book is filled with practical exercises and techniques for cultivating mindfulness and self-awareness, such as paying attention to the breath, observing our thoughts without judgment, and letting go of negative emotions. Tolle emphasizes the importance of surrendering to the present moment and accepting things as they are, rather than constantly struggling against them.

Throughout the book, Tolle draws on a wide range of spiritual traditions, from Zen Buddhism to Christian mysticism, to illustrate his points. He emphasizes that the ultimate goal of spiritual practice is not to attain some higher state of consciousness or to escape the world but to become fully present and alive in the here and now.

Overall, The Power of Now is a powerful and inspiring guidebook for anyone seeking to cultivate greater self-awareness, inner peace, and spiritual fulfillment in their lives

CHAPTER 10

Health and Wellness

46.   The 4-Hour Body by Timothy Ferriss

Quotes

"The body is a machine, and we can hack the machine to make it perform better and achieve our goals faster."

"Small changes in behavior can lead to big results. You don't need to make radical changes to see significant improvements in your health and fitness."

"The key to successful weight loss is not dieting, but making sustainable lifestyle changes that you can stick to in the long term."

"Resistance training is the most effective way to build muscle and burn fat, and should be a part of everyone's fitness routine."

"There is no one-size-fits-all approach to nutrition. You need to experiment and find what works best for your body."

"Sleep is essential for recovery and overall health. Prioritize getting enough quality sleep every night."

"Hormones play a critical role in our health and fitness, and we can manipulate them through nutrition, exercise, and other lifestyle factors."

"The mind is just as important as the body when it comes to achieving our goals. We need to cultivate a growth mindset and stay motivated through challenges."

"It's important to measure progress and track data to see what's working and what's not. This helps us make informed decisions about our health and fitness."

"There are no shortcuts or magic pills when it comes to health and fitness. It takes hard work, consistency, and patience to achieve lasting results."

Lessons

You can achieve significant results with minimal effort: The book emphasizes the importance of using scientific principles and efficient techniques to achieve maximum results with minimal effort. This means focusing on the most effective exercises, diets, and lifestyle changes, rather than spending hours on less effective activities.

Consistency is key: While quick results are certainly possible, the book also emphasizes the importance of consistency and long-term commitment. Building healthy habits and sticking to them over time is essential for achieving lasting results.

Personalization is important: Everyone's body is unique, and what works for one person may not work for another. The book emphasizes the importance of experimenting and personalizing your approach to fitness, nutrition, and lifestyle in order to find what works best for you.

Tracking progress is crucial: In order to make progress towards your goals, it's important to track your progress and make adjustments as needed. The book provides tools and techniques for tracking everything from body composition to sleep quality, to help you stay on track and make informed decisions.

Small changes can make a big difference: Rather than trying to make sweeping changes all at once, the book emphasizes the power of making small, incremental changes that can add up to big results over time. This can help you avoid overwhelm and build healthy habits that last.

Mindset is key: The book emphasizes the importance of developing a growth mindset and believing in your own ability to achieve your goals. It also emphasizes the importance of addressing any mental barriers or limiting beliefs that may be holding you back.

Prioritization is crucial: With so many competing demands on our time and energy, it's important to prioritize the things that truly matter. The book emphasizes the importance of identifying your priorities and focusing your time and energy on the activities that will move you closer to your goals.

Summary

"The 4-Hour Body" by Timothy Ferriss is a comprehensive guide to achieving optimal health and fitness with minimal time and effort. The book provides practical advice and techniques for everything from losing fat and gaining muscle to improving sleep quality and increasing athletic performance. Ferriss emphasizes the importance of using scientific principles and personalization to achieve maximum results with minimal effort. He also emphasizes the importance of consistency, tracking progress, and developing a growth mindset in order to achieve lasting results. The book provides a wealth of information and resources for anyone looking to improve their health and fitness, and encourages readers to experiment and find what works best for their unique bodies and lifestyles.

47.   The Paleo Solution by Robb Wolf

Quotes

"We have not evolved to eat grains, beans, and other legumes, or dairy products, and consuming them can cause health problems."

"The food pyramid and USDA recommendations are not based on sound science, and are contributing to the obesity epidemic and other chronic diseases."

"Our ancestors ate a diet high in animal protein, healthy fats, and fruits and vegetables, which is what our bodies are designed to thrive on."

"Processed foods and modern agricultural practices have drastically changed the nutrient content of our food, and are contributing to chronic diseases like diabetes, heart disease, and cancer."

"Following a Paleo diet can improve your energy levels, help you lose weight, and reduce your risk of chronic diseases."

"Physical activity is crucial for our health and well-being, and should be a regular part of our daily routine."

"Sleep is essential for optimal health, and chronic sleep deprivation can contribute to a range of health problems."

"Stress is a major contributor to chronic diseases, and managing stress through techniques like meditation, yoga, or simply taking time to relax is important for our health."

"The Paleo diet is not a fad, but a return to the way our ancestors ate for millions of years, and can be a sustainable way of eating for life."

"The key to optimal health is not just diet or exercise, but a combination of factors including nutrition, physical activity, sleep, stress management, and social support."

Lessons

Our modern diet and lifestyle is at odds with our evolutionary history, which can contribute to chronic health issues like obesity, diabetes, and heart disease. By adopting a Paleo lifestyle that aligns with our genetic makeup, we can better support our health and reduce our risk of chronic disease.

Processed foods are a major contributor to chronic disease, and reducing our intake of these foods is critical for optimal health outcomes.

Eating whole, nutrient-dense foods is key to achieving optimal health and performance, and should be prioritized over processed, nutrient-poor foods.

Exercise is a critical component of a healthy lifestyle, but it cannot compensate for a poor diet that is high in processed foods.

Sleep is a critical component of overall health and well-being, and should be prioritized just as much as nutrition and exercise.

The Paleo lifestyle is a holistic approach to health and wellness that prioritizes not just diet, but also sleep, exercise, and stress reduction.

The Paleo lifestyle is not about deprivation, but rather about eating delicious, satisfying foods that nourish the body and promote health.

By adopting a Paleo lifestyle, we can improve our health, reduce our risk of chronic disease, and live a longer, more fulfilling life.

Summary

"The Paleo Solution" by Robb Wolf is a comprehensive guide to adopting a Paleo lifestyle, which is based on the idea that our modern diet and lifestyle are at odds with our evolutionary history, leading to chronic health issues like obesity, diabetes, and heart disease. The book provides a thorough overview of the science behind the Paleo lifestyle, including the benefits of eating whole, nutrient-dense foods and the negative effects of processed foods. It also emphasizes the importance of exercise, sleep, and stress reduction in achieving optimal health outcomes. The book provides practical advice on how to adopt a Paleo lifestyle, including meal planning and preparation tips, exercise recommendations, and strategies for reducing stress. Overall, "The Paleo Solution" offers a holistic approach to health and wellness that can help readers improve their health, reduce their risk of chronic disease, and live a longer, more fulfilling life.

48. The Whole30 by Melissa Hartwig and Dallas Hartwig

Quotes

"This is not hard. Don't you dare tell us this is hard. Quitting heroin is hard. Beating cancer is hard. Drinking your coffee black. Is. Not. Hard."

"We cannot change everything in our lives overnight, but we can change one thing today. One decision, one positive action, one healthy choice."

"We're not talking about a diet; we're talking about a lifestyle change. The Whole30 is about redefining how you think about food and how you live your life."

"The food you eat either makes you more healthy or less healthy. Those are your options."

"The Whole30 is not a magic solution for everyone, but it is a magic solution for many."

"The foods you eat, the amount you sleep, the stress you experience, and the amount and type of physical activity you engage in all play a role in your overall health."

"It is not just about the food you eat; it is also about the food you don't eat. The Whole30 eliminates foods that are known to cause inflammation, hormonal disruption, and gut dysbiosis."

"We have a choice: to eat foods that support our health or foods that harm our health. The Whole30 is about making that choice consciously and intentionally."

"The Whole30 is not about perfection, it's about progress. Every healthy choice you make is a step in the right direction."

"Change happens one day at a time, one meal at a time, one choice at a time."

Lessons

Your food choices have a significant impact on your health: The Whole30 emphasizes the importance of eating nutrient-dense whole foods and avoiding foods that can cause inflammation, hormonal disruption, and gut dysbiosis.

The Whole30 is not a quick fix: This program is designed to be a lifestyle change, not a short-term diet. It requires a commitment to making healthier choices and developing sustainable habits.

Self-experimentation is important: The Whole30 encourages individuals to pay attention to how different foods make them feel, both physically and emotionally. This can help them identify food sensitivities and intolerances.

Mindset is key: The Whole30 emphasizes the importance of developing a positive mindset and reframing the way you think about food and health. It encourages individuals to focus on progress, not perfection.

Support is essential: The Whole30 encourages individuals to seek support from family, friends, and a community of like-minded individuals to help them stay on track and maintain their motivation.

Lifestyle factors beyond food impact your health: The Whole30 emphasizes the importance of getting enough sleep, managing stress, and engaging in regular physical activity to support overall health.

Small changes can make a big difference: The Whole30 encourages individuals to start with small changes and build momentum over time. Even making one healthy choice per day can lead to significant improvements in health over time.

Summary

"The Whole30" by Melissa Hartwig and Dallas Hartwig is a guidebook and program for a 30-day dietary and lifestyle reset. The book focuses on the importance of eating nutrient-dense whole foods while avoiding foods that can cause inflammation, hormonal disruption, and gut dysbiosis. The program emphasizes self-experimentation, positive mindset, and the importance of community support. In addition to dietary changes, the book also encourages individuals to prioritize lifestyle factors such as sleep, stress management, and physical activity. Overall, "The Whole30" aims to help individuals develop healthier habits and achieve sustainable improvements in their health and well-being.

49. The Blue Zones by Dan Buettner

Quotes

"The way people in Blue Zones live is sustainable and fulfilling. They don't have to rely on the type of technology and medicine that we do in the West."

"The most important thing you can do to live a long life is to have a sense of purpose."

"In the Blue Zones, people don't just survive, they thrive. They enjoy life, have close-knit families and communities, and feel a sense of purpose in their daily lives."

"The key to longevity is not just about what you eat or how much you exercise, but also about your social connections and sense of belonging."

"In the Blue Zones, people eat mostly plant-based diets, and they also enjoy moderate amounts of alcohol and caffeine."

"One of the most important factors in the Blue Zones is the strong sense of community and social support. People are surrounded by friends and family who care about them and help them when they need it."

"People in Blue Zones don't just focus on physical health, but also on mental and emotional health. They practice relaxation techniques and have a positive outlook on life."

"The lesson from the Blue Zones is that we don't need to rely on expensive drugs and medical procedures to live long and healthy lives. We just need to adopt a lifestyle that supports our health and well-being."

Lessons

Eat a Plant-Based Diet: People in Blue Zones eat mostly plant-based diets that are rich in fruits, vegetables, whole grains, and legumes. They consume small amounts of meat and fish, and limit their intake of processed foods and sugary drinks.

Move Naturally: Blue Zone residents move their bodies naturally throughout the day, by walking, gardening, and doing household chores. They don't go to the gym or do structured exercise, but rather incorporate movement into their daily lives.

Cultivate a Sense of Purpose: People in Blue Zones have a strong sense of purpose in their lives, which helps them to stay motivated and engaged. They have clear goals, a reason to wake up in the morning, and a sense of belonging to a community.

Connect with Others: People in Blue Zones have strong social connections with friends and family. They have close-knit communities that support them and provide them with a sense of belonging.

Practice Stress Reduction: People in Blue Zones practice stress reduction techniques, such as meditation, prayer, or napping. They also take time to relax and enjoy life, and have a positive outlook on the world.

Enjoy Moderate Amounts of Alcohol: People in Blue Zones enjoy moderate amounts of alcohol, usually in the form of red wine. They drink in moderation and often with friends and family, which helps to foster a sense of community.

Have a Strong Support System: People in Blue Zones have strong support systems, including friends, family, and community members. They are surrounded by people who care about them and are willing to help them in times of need.

Prioritize Rest: People in Blue Zones prioritize rest and get enough sleep each night. They also take time to relax and unwind throughout the day, which helps them to reduce stress and feel more centered.

Overall, the lessons from "The Blue Zones" suggest that living a long and healthy life is not just about diet and exercise, but also about social connections, sense of purpose, and stress reduction. By adopting these practices, we can improve our health and well-being and increase our chances of living a long and fulfilling life.

Summary

"The Blue Zones" by Dan Buettner is a book that examines the lifestyles and habits of the world's healthiest and longest-lived people. Buettner identifies five regions, or "blue zones," around the world where people live significantly longer and healthier lives than the average person. These regions are Okinawa, Japan; Sardinia, Italy; Nicoya, Costa Rica; Icaria, Greece; and Loma Linda, California.

Through his research, Buettner identifies nine commonalities that are shared among these communities, including plant-based diets, natural movement, a sense of purpose, social connections, stress reduction, moderate alcohol intake, strong support systems, prioritizing rest, and a focus on family and community.

Buettner also provides practical tips for incorporating these habits into your own life, as well as sharing stories of individuals who have successfully adopted these practices and have seen significant improvements in their health and well-being.

Overall, "The Blue Zones" provides valuable insights into how we can improve our health and longevity by adopting the lifestyles and habits of the world's healthiest and longest-lived people.

50. The Bulletproof Diet by Dave Asprey

Quotes

"The Bulletproof Diet is a highly effective, science-based approach to nutrition that helps you lose weight, increase energy, and feel better than ever."

"Eating the right foods at the right time can turn on your fat-burning metabolism, control your cravings, and help you feel energized all day long."

"Bulletproof coffee is the ultimate way to power up your morning, providing sustained energy and mental clarity without the crash or jitters of traditional coffee."

"The Bulletproof Diet is not about deprivation or counting calories – it's about eating delicious, nutrient-dense foods that help your body thrive."

"By eliminating toxins and inflammatory foods, you can reduce inflammation, boost your immune system, and optimize your health."

"Bulletproof intermittent fasting is a powerful tool for weight loss, energy, and mental clarity – it's like hitting the reset button on your body."

"Sleep is one of the most important components of overall health, and by optimizing your sleep environment and habits, you can improve your energy, mood, and productivity."

"The Bulletproof Diet is not a one-size-fits-all approach – it's about finding what works best for your unique body and lifestyle."

"By focusing on quality over quantity, and listening to your body's signals, you can create a sustainable, lifelong approach to health and wellness."

"The Bulletproof Diet is a roadmap to optimal health and vitality, providing you with the tools and knowledge you need to take control of your health and transform your life."

Lessons

The importance of eating nutrient-dense foods: The Bulletproof Diet emphasizes the importance of eating whole, nutrient-dense foods that provide your body with the vitamins and minerals it needs to function at its best.

The impact of toxins on the body: The book explains how toxins in our food and environment can contribute to inflammation and other health problems, and provides guidance on how to minimize our exposure to toxins.

The benefits of intermittent fasting: The Bulletproof Diet introduces the concept of intermittent fasting and explains how it can help boost weight loss, energy levels, and mental clarity.

The value of high-quality fats: The book encourages the consumption of high-quality fats, such as those found in grass-fed butter and coconut oil, and explains how these fats can provide sustained energy and other health benefits.

The importance of optimizing sleep: The Bulletproof Diet emphasizes the importance of getting high-quality sleep, and provides guidance on how to create a sleep environment and establish habits that promote restful sleep.

The value of personalized nutrition: The book emphasizes the importance of finding what works best for your unique body and lifestyle, and provides guidance on how to personalize your nutrition and exercise plan for optimal results.

The role of mindset in achieving health goals: The Bulletproof Diet encourages readers to adopt a growth mindset, focus on progress rather than perfection, and approach health and wellness as a lifelong journey rather than a short-term goal.

Summary

The Bulletproof Diet by Dave Asprey is a guide to optimal nutrition and health, based on the idea that eating the right foods at the right time can help you lose weight, increase energy, and improve overall wellbeing. The book emphasizes the importance of nutrient-dense foods, high-quality fats, and intermittent fasting, and provides guidance on how to minimize exposure to toxins and optimize sleep for optimal health. The Bulletproof Diet is not a one-size-fits-all approach, but rather a personalized plan based on individual needs and preferences. The book also emphasizes the importance of adopting a growth mindset, focusing on progress rather than perfection, and approaching health and wellness as a lifelong journey. Overall, the Bulletproof Diet is a roadmap to optimal health and vitality, providing readers with the tools and knowledge they need to take control of their health and transform their lives.

CHAPTER 11
Success in Relationships

51. Crucial Conversations: Tools for Talking When Stakes Are High by Kerry Patterson, Joseph Grenny, Ron McMillan, and Al Switzler

Quotes

"People who are skilled at dialogue do their best to make it safe for everyone to add their meaning to the shared pool--even ideas that at first glance appear controversial, wrong, or at odds with their own beliefs. Now, obviously they don't agree with every idea; they simply do their best to ensure that all ideas find their way into the open."

"The moment a crucial conversation turns from a healthy debate to a personal attack, the discussion is no longer about the original purpose--it's now about defending one's honor."

"We all have our own filters that we see the world through. We need to be aware of those filters and try to take them into account when we're having conversations with others."

"The single most important thing you can do to improve your relationships is to make the shift from figuring out who's right to figuring out what's right."

"When we're under stress, we can fall back on habits that don't serve us well. One of those habits is to stop listening and become defensive. We need to recognize when we're feeling defensive and make a conscious effort to stay open to other perspectives."

"When emotions run high, people are more likely to make bad decisions. It's important to take a step back, cool down, and approach the conversation with a clear head."

"The key to making crucial conversations work is to help others feel safe enough to share what they're thinking and feeling. When people feel safe, they're more likely to be open and honest."

"Silence can be just as damaging to a relationship as harsh words. When we withhold our thoughts and feelings, we're not being honest with ourselves or the other person."

"We often focus on the words that are being said in a conversation, but body language and tone of voice are just as important. We need to be aware of our own body language and tone, as well as the other person's, to really understand the conversation."

"Crucial conversations are not about winning or losing. They're about finding a way to work together to achieve a common goal."

Lessons

Identify and understand the importance of crucial conversations: Crucial conversations are those discussions that are emotionally charged, where opinions differ, and the stakes are high. Identifying these conversations and understanding their importance can help you prepare for them better.

Master your emotions: During crucial conversations, it is essential to keep your emotions in check. Take a moment to reflect and get in the right state of mind before engaging in the conversation.

Focus on the issue, not the person: Avoid personal attacks and instead focus on the issue at hand. Stick to the facts and avoid making assumptions about the other person's intentions.

Listen actively: Effective communication involves active listening. Listen with an open mind and try to understand the other person's perspective. Encourage them to share their thoughts and feelings.

Speak honestly: Be honest in your communication, even if it's uncomfortable. Speak clearly and directly, without attacking or blaming the other person.

Look for mutual purpose: In crucial conversations, it's important to look for mutual purpose. Find common ground and work towards a solution that benefits everyone involved.

Create safety: Establish an environment of safety and trust in the conversation. Encourage openness and honesty, and avoid making people feel attacked or defensive.

Practice dialogue: Dialogue is the art of turning crucial conversations into meaningful discussions. Practice the skills of dialogue to improve your communication in difficult situations.

Use the tools provided: The book provides a range of tools and techniques for effective communication in crucial conversations. Practice and implement these tools to improve your communication skills.

Continuously improve: Effective communication is a skill that requires continuous improvement. Reflect on your communication after crucial conversations and identify areas for improvement.

Summary

"Crucial Conversations: Tools for Talking When Stakes Are High" by Kerry Patterson, Joseph Grenny, Ron McMillan, and Al Switzler is a guidebook for navigating difficult conversations. The book explores how to handle conversations that are emotionally charged, where opinions differ, and the stakes are high. It provides tools and techniques for effective communication, focusing on identifying and understanding crucial conversations, mastering emotions, listening actively, speaking honestly, creating safety, practicing dialogue, and continuously improving communication skills.

The book emphasizes the importance of identifying crucial conversations and understanding their significance. It highlights the role of emotions in communication and provides techniques for managing them. It emphasizes active listening and honest communication, focusing on the issue at hand rather than the person. It also explores the importance of creating safety in conversations and finding mutual purpose.

The book provides a range of tools and techniques for effective communication, including techniques for creating safety, asking questions to encourage dialogue, and exploring different perspectives. It emphasizes the importance of practice and continuous improvement, providing exercises and tips for improving communication skills.

Overall, "Crucial Conversations" is a practical guidebook for anyone looking to improve their communication skills in difficult situations. It provides concrete tools and techniques for navigating emotionally charged conversations and finding common ground, allowing for more productive and effective communication.

52. Men Are from Mars, Women Are from Venus by John Gray

Quotes

"Men are motivated when they feel needed while women are motivated when they feel cherished."

"Men become more distant and non-communicative, not because they do not care, but because they are afraid of saying something wrong and making the situation worse."

"Women tend to take problems to heart and worry about them, while men tend to withdraw and become engrossed in other activities."

"When a woman tells a man about a problem she is having, she is usually looking for empathy and support, not solutions. Men, on the other hand, often make the mistake of offering solutions when all the woman really wants is a sympathetic ear."

"Men are like rubber bands. They pull away and then come back. Women are like waves. They move up and down in their moods and their levels of intimacy."

"When a man can listen to a woman's feelings without getting angry and frustrated, he gives her a wonderful gift. He makes it safe for her to express herself."

"Men want to feel trusted and appreciated. Women want to feel cherished and understood."

"Women need to feel that their emotions are understood and valued, while men need to feel that their solutions are valued and respected."

"Women often give too much to others and not enough to themselves, while men often focus too much on themselves and not enough on others."

"By understanding and accepting the differences between men and women, we can learn to communicate more effectively and create stronger, more loving relationships."

Lessons

Men and women are fundamentally different in the way they communicate, think, and behave. Understanding and accepting these differences is crucial to building strong and healthy relationships.

Men and women have different needs and priorities in relationships. Men need to feel respected and appreciated, while women need to feel loved and understood.

Men and women have different ways of dealing with stress and problems. Men tend to withdraw and seek solitude, while women seek emotional support and communication.

Men and women have different communication styles. Men tend to be more direct and solutions-focused, while women tend to be more indirect and relationship-focused.

Men and women have different ways of expressing love and affection. Men tend to show love through actions, while women tend to show love through words and gestures.

Successful relationships require effort and compromise from both partners. Each partner must be willing to understand and accept the other's differences, and work together to build a strong and loving relationship.

It's important to communicate openly and honestly in relationships, and to express your needs and feelings in a clear and respectful manner.

A relationship should be a source of joy, support, and fulfillment for both partners. It's important to make time for each other, show appreciation and affection, and work together to build a happy and fulfilling life together.

Summary

"Men Are from Mars, Women Are from Venus" by John Gray is a book that explores the fundamental differences between men and women in relationships. Gray argues that men and women have different communication styles, priorities, and ways of dealing with stress and problems. He suggests that understanding and accepting these differences is essential for building strong and healthy relationships.

The book offers insights into the male and female psyche, explaining why men and women often have difficulty understanding each other. Gray provides practical advice on how to improve communication, manage conflicts, and create more fulfilling relationships. He also emphasizes the importance of expressing love and affection, and making time for each other in a busy world.

Overall, "Men Are from Mars, Women Are from Venus" is a guide for both men and women to navigate the complex world of relationships. It encourages couples to embrace their differences, communicate openly and honestly, and work together to build a happy and fulfilling life together.

53. The 5 Love Languages for Men/Women by Gary Chapman

Quotes

"The key to a successful marriage is choosing to love your spouse every day, and learning how to express that love in a way that speaks to them."

"When we speak our spouse's love language, we make deposits into their emotional love tank, which helps keep the relationship strong and healthy."

"One of the biggest mistakes men make in their marriages is assuming that their wives think and feel the same way they do. We have to learn to understand and appreciate our wives' unique perspectives and emotions."

"Acts of service are a powerful way to communicate love to your spouse. When you do something helpful or thoughtful for your wife, it shows her that you care about her needs and well-being."

"Physical touch is a vital aspect of a healthy marriage. For many men, physical touch is their primary love language, and they feel most loved and connected when their wives initiate physical affection."

From "The 5 Love Languages for Women":

"In a healthy marriage, both partners should feel loved and appreciated for who they are. When we learn to speak our husband's love language, we show him that we accept and value him just as he is."

"Gift-giving is a powerful way to express love, but it's not just about the material item itself. It's about the thought and effort that went into choosing the gift, and the message it communicates: 'I know you, I understand you, and I care about you.'"

"Words of affirmation can have a tremendous impact on a man's self-esteem and sense of worth. When we praise and encourage our husbands, we help them feel valued and appreciated, which strengthens the bond between us."

"Quality time is a precious commodity in our busy lives, but it's essential for building and maintaining strong relationships. When we prioritize time with our husbands, we show them that they are a priority in our lives."

"Physical touch is a fundamental aspect of human connection and intimacy. When we initiate physical affection with our husbands, we show them that we desire and appreciate them on a deep level."

Lessons

Understanding your spouse's love language is essential for a healthy and fulfilling relationship. The book explains that everyone has a primary way of giving and receiving love, and it's important to identify and express love in the way that speaks to your spouse.

Love is an action, not just a feeling. Love requires intentional effort and action, and expressing love in your spouse's preferred love language is a powerful way to demonstrate your love and commitment.

Communication is key in any relationship. The book emphasizes the importance of open and honest communication, especially when it comes to expressing needs and desires.

Marriage requires constant effort and attention. The author stresses the need for ongoing effort and investment in a relationship, including regularly expressing love and appreciation, making time for each other, and continuing to learn and grow together.

Different genders may have different love languages. While the love languages are universal, the book acknowledges that there may be differences in how men and women tend to give and receive love. Understanding these differences can help couples navigate their relationship more effectively.

Overall, "The 5 Love Languages for Men/Women" emphasizes the importance of learning to love and communicate in a way that speaks to your spouse, and working together to build a strong and fulfilling relationship.

Summary

"The 5 Love Languages for Men/Women" by Gary Chapman is a book that explores the concept of love languages and how they can be used to improve relationships between couples. The book outlines five primary love languages: words of affirmation, acts of service, receiving gifts, quality time, and physical touch. The author explains that everyone has a primary love language, and understanding and expressing love in this language is essential for a healthy and fulfilling relationship.

The book is divided into two parts, one for men and one for women, and explores how each gender can use the love languages to improve their relationship with their partner. The author emphasizes the importance of communication, understanding, and ongoing effort in building and maintaining a strong and healthy relationship.

Overall, "The 5 Love Languages for Men/Women" provides practical guidance and tools for couples looking to improve their relationship and deepen their connection with each other. By learning to speak each other's love language, couples can build a stronger foundation for a fulfilling and lasting relationship.

54. The Art of Loving by Erich Fromm

Quotes

"Love is an art, just as living is an art; if we want to learn how to love we must proceed in the same way we have to proceed if we want to learn any other art, say music, painting, carpentry, or the art of medicine or engineering."

"Immature love says: 'I love you because I need you.' Mature love says: 'I need you because I love you.'"

"Love is not primarily a relationship to a specific person; it is an attitude, an orientation of character which determines the relatedness of a person to the world as a whole, not toward one 'object' of love."

"The task we must set for ourselves is not to feel secure, but to be able to tolerate insecurity."

"The capacity to love is determined by one's own level of evolution."

"The most fundamental kind of love, which underlies all types of love, is brotherly love."

"To love somebody is not just a strong feeling—it is a decision, it is a judgment, it is a promise."

"Love isn't something natural. Rather, it requires discipline, concentration, patience, faith, and the overcoming of narcissism. It isn't a feeling, it is a practice."

"Love means to commit oneself without guarantee, to give oneself completely in the hope that our love will produce love in the loved person. Love is an act of faith, and whoever is of little faith is also of little love."

"The art of loving is the art of knowing how to combine these two ingredients: to be able to express one's own innermost being, and to be able to respond to the other's."

"The only way of knowing a person is to love them without hope of reward or fear of punishment."

"Love is often nothing but a favorable exchange between two people who get the most of what they can expect, considering their value on the personality market."

Lessons

Love is an art that requires learning and practice, just like any other art. We need to be committed to learning about ourselves and others to develop the capacity for love.

Love is not just a feeling, but a decision and a commitment to another person. We must choose to love someone and make a promise to commit to them.

True love is not based on our own needs or desires, but rather a genuine concern and care for the well-being of the other person. We must be willing to give and sacrifice for the other person.

Love requires discipline, patience, and overcoming our own narcissism. We need to be self-aware and willing to work on our own flaws and insecurities to truly love another person.

We must be able to express our own innermost being while also being receptive to the other person. This requires open communication, honesty, and vulnerability.

Love is a fundamental human need, and our capacity to love is determined by our level of emotional and psychological development.

We must be willing to tolerate insecurity and uncertainty to truly love someone. Love requires risk and the willingness to embrace vulnerability.

Love is not just a personal relationship, but an attitude and orientation towards the world. We must cultivate a sense of brotherly love and compassion towards all people to truly live a loving life.

Finally, love is an act of faith. We cannot guarantee that our love will be reciprocated or that we will not be hurt, but we must have faith in the power of love to transform our lives and the lives of those around us.

Summary

The Art of Loving by Erich Fromm is a philosophical exploration of what it means to truly love another person. Fromm argues that love is an art that requires learning, discipline, and practice, rather than just a feeling or emotion. He contends that our modern society often confuses love with possessiveness, and that we must learn to cultivate a genuine concern and care for the well-being of the other person to truly love.

Fromm explores different types of love, including motherly love, brotherly love, and erotic love, and emphasizes that all types of love require a selfless commitment to the other person. He also discusses the psychological and emotional development necessary to develop the capacity for love, including self-awareness, the ability to tolerate insecurity and uncertainty, and the willingness to overcome our own narcissism.

Throughout the book, Fromm stresses the importance of open communication, honesty, and vulnerability in relationships, as well as the need for a sense of brotherly love and compassion towards all people. Ultimately, he argues that love is an act of faith, and that by cultivating the art of loving, we can transform our lives and the lives of those around us.

55. Attached: The New Science of Adult Attachment and How It Can Help You Find and Keep Love by Amir Levine and Rachel S. F. Heller

Quotes

"Attachment theory offers a new lens through which we can understand our most intimate relationships--not just romantic ones, but those with our parents, children, and close friends as well."

"In a healthy relationship, each partner's attachment system can support the other's. When one person feels insecure, the other can provide comfort and reassurance."

"In an insecure relationship, the anxious partner is preoccupied with the relationship, while the avoidant partner tends to withdraw and shut down emotionally."

"The key to finding and maintaining love is to understand our attachment style and that of our partner, and to learn how to communicate effectively and meet each other's needs."

"Our attachment style is not set in stone. With self-awareness and effort, we can develop a more secure attachment style and create more fulfilling relationships."

"The more we understand our own attachment style, the better equipped we are to find a partner who can meet our needs and communicate effectively with them."

"People with a secure attachment style tend to have better self-esteem, be more resilient in the face of stress, and have more satisfying relationships overall."

"By recognizing and working on our attachment patterns, we can develop a more positive and healthy sense of self, and create more fulfilling relationships with others."

Lessons

Understand your attachment style: The book emphasizes the importance of understanding your own attachment style and how it impacts your relationships. It identifies three attachment styles: secure, anxious, and avoidant.

Communication is key: Effective communication is crucial in any relationship. The book suggests that partners with different attachment styles may have difficulty communicating effectively, but by recognizing and understanding these differences, they can learn to communicate better.

Find a compatible partner: The book suggests that finding a partner with a compatible attachment style can lead to a more fulfilling relationship. It recommends that individuals with an anxious attachment style look for partners with a secure attachment style, while those with an avoidant attachment style may benefit from a partner who is secure or less avoidant.

Learn to become more secure: The book acknowledges that attachment styles can change and that individuals can learn to become more secure. It suggests that developing self-awareness, practicing self-care, and working on communication skills can help individuals move towards a more secure attachment style.

Be mindful of patterns: The book suggests that individuals should be mindful of patterns in their relationships and take steps to avoid negative patterns. For example, someone with an anxious attachment style may tend to pursue partners who are avoidant, leading to a cycle of anxious-avoidant relationships.

Take responsibility for your own happiness: The book emphasizes the importance of taking responsibility for your own happiness and well-being, rather than relying on a partner to fulfill all your needs. It suggests that individuals should focus on developing their own self-esteem and self-care practices, rather than seeking validation from a partner.

Seek professional help if needed: Finally, the book acknowledges that some individuals may need professional help to address issues related to attachment styles and relationship patterns. It suggests seeking out a therapist or counselor who is familiar with attachment theory and can provide guidance and support.

Summary

Attached: The New Science of Adult Attachment and How It Can Help You Find and Keep Love by Amir Levine and Rachel S. F. Heller is a book that explores attachment theory and how it can be used to understand adult relationships. The authors describe three main attachment styles - secure, anxious, and avoidant - and explain how they impact our behaviors and emotions in relationships.

The book emphasizes the importance of understanding your own attachment style and that of your partner, and learning how to communicate effectively to meet each other's needs. It provides strategies for developing a more secure attachment style, including self-awareness, self-care, and working on communication skills.

The authors suggest that finding a compatible partner with a compatible attachment style can lead to a more fulfilling relationship. They also encourage individuals to take responsibility for their own happiness and well-being, rather than relying on a partner to fulfill all their needs.

Overall, Attached provides practical insights and advice for anyone looking to improve their relationships or find and keep love. By understanding attachment theory and working to develop a more secure attachment style, readers can create more fulfilling and satisfying relationships with themselves and others.

CHAPTER 12

Spirituality and Mindfulness

56. The Power of Intention by Wayne W. Dyer

Quotes

"When you trust in yourself, you are trusting in the wisdom that created you."

"The greatest gift you were ever given is your imagination. Within it is the power to create a world of your own."

"When you are able to shift your inner awareness to how you can serve others, and when you make this the central focus of your life, you will then be in a position to know true miracles in your progress toward prosperity."

"The power of intention is the power to manifest, to create, to live a life of unlimited abundance, and to attract into your life the right people at the right moments."

"You cannot always control what goes on outside. But you can always control what goes on inside."

"The more you see yourself as what you'd like to become, and act as if what you want is already there, the more you'll activate those dormant forces that will collaborate to transform your dream into your reality."

"Your imagination is your preview of life's coming attractions."

"When you're at peace with yourself and love your self, it is virtually impossible to do things to yourself that are destructive."

"The purpose of life is a life of purpose."

"Intention is not something you do, but rather a force that exists in the universe as an invisible field of energy."

Lessons

Your thoughts and intentions shape your reality: According to the book, the power of intention is the key to manifesting your desires and creating a fulfilling life. By focusing on positive thoughts and setting clear intentions, you can attract the experiences, people, and circumstances that align with your goals and values.

Cultivate a strong sense of purpose: The book emphasizes the importance of living a purpose-driven life. When you have a clear sense of your values and goals, you can channel your energy and intentions toward achieving what truly matters to you.

Connect with your inner wisdom: The author suggests that by connecting with your inner wisdom, you can tap into the universal intelligence that guides and supports all of us. By cultivating a deep sense of trust in yourself and the universe, you can manifest your intentions with ease and grace.

Practice mindfulness and presence: The book encourages readers to be fully present and engaged in each moment. By focusing on the present moment and letting go of worries about the future or regrets about the past, you can cultivate a sense of inner peace and alignment with your intentions.

Cultivate a positive attitude: The author suggests that a positive attitude is key to living a happy, fulfilling life. By focusing on the good in yourself and others, you can attract more positivity and abundance into your life.

Take inspired action: The book emphasizes the importance of taking action toward your goals, but not just any action. The author suggests taking action that is inspired by your intuition and inner wisdom, rather than just following a set of prescribed steps or strategies.

Trust the process: Finally, the book encourages readers to trust the process of life and the universe. By letting go of attachment to specific outcomes and trusting that everything is unfolding as it should, you can relax into the flow of life and allow your intentions to manifest in their own time and way.

Summary

"The Power of Intention" by Wayne W. Dyer is a self-help book that emphasizes the importance of harnessing the power of intention to create a fulfilling life. According to the author, intention is the force that shapes our reality and enables us to manifest our desires. The book offers practical advice and exercises for cultivating a strong sense of purpose, connecting with your inner wisdom, practicing mindfulness and presence, cultivating a positive attitude, taking inspired action, and trusting the process of life. The author also emphasizes the importance of living a purpose-driven life and connecting with the universal intelligence that guides and supports all of us. Overall, the book encourages readers to live with intention and align their thoughts, actions, and energy with their deepest values and goals.

57. The Celestine Prophecy by James Redfield

Quotes

"We must assume every event has significance and contains a message that pertains to our questions...this especially applies to what we used to call bad things...the challenge is to find the silver lining in every event, no matter how negative."

"The coincidences that happen in your life; the events, the people, the experiences that seem to arrive at just the right time...are whispers from the universe, encouraging you to follow your intuition, your hunches, your gut."

"The secret of joy in work is contained in one word - excellence. To know how to do something well is to enjoy it."

"The first step in authentic spiritual growth is to realize that our egos are the source of all our troubles."

"We begin to notice, therefore, that coincidences are flowing through our lives all the time. When we recognize that they are flowing, and then consciously act on them, they are in essence providing us with a glimpse of the unity that underlies all things."

"When we stop opposing reality, action becomes simple, fluid, kind, and fearless."

"Every struggle is a lesson, and there's no point in beating yourself up over a failure. Plan for it, learn from it, and move on to the next adventure."

"We're not just blindly thrown by our circumstances; we're propelled by them. We're part of something larger than ourselves, and we're here for a reason."

"We must learn to break the habitual pattern of thought, to look beyond the ideas that we have been taught, and learn to see things in a different way."

"We can never fully realize the joy inherent in life until we learn to practice forgiveness."

Lessons

The universe communicates with us through meaningful coincidences, and we can learn to recognize and act on these synchronicities to enhance our spiritual growth.

There is a deeper meaning and purpose behind every event in our lives, even those that seem negative, and we can learn to interpret them as opportunities for growth.

Our egos are often the source of our problems, and we can cultivate greater self-awareness and humility to overcome them.

Our thoughts and beliefs shape our reality, and we can learn to break free from limiting beliefs and see the world in a new way.

Forgiveness is a powerful tool for healing and releasing negative emotions.

We are all interconnected, and our actions have a ripple effect that can impact others and the world around us.

Following our intuition and living in alignment with our true selves is key to finding fulfillment and purpose in life.

Fear and resistance can hold us back from experiencing our full potential, and we must learn to overcome them.

By practicing presence, gratitude, and kindness, we can cultivate greater happiness and fulfillment in our lives.

Spiritual growth is an ongoing journey that requires commitment and perseverance, but the rewards are immeasurable.

Summary

"The Celestine Prophecy" by James Redfield is a spiritual novel that follows the journey of a man named John as he travels to Peru in search of a mysterious manuscript that reveals nine insights into the nature of reality and the evolution of human consciousness.

Throughout his journey, John encounters a series of synchronistic events and encounters that lead him to uncover each of the insights, which include understanding the interconnectedness of all things, breaking free from limiting beliefs and patterns, and cultivating greater self-awareness and spiritual connection.

Along the way, John also learns about the power of intuition, forgiveness, and gratitude, and the importance of living in alignment with one's true purpose and values. He also faces challenges from those who seek to keep the insights hidden and must learn to overcome his own fears and resistance in order to fully embrace the spiritual journey.

"The Celestine Prophecy" ultimately presents a vision of a world transformed by the evolution of human consciousness, and encourages readers to take an active role in contributing to this evolution by cultivating their own spiritual growth and living in harmony with others and the natural world.

58. The Alchemist by Paulo Coelho

Quotes

"And, when you want something, all the universe conspires in helping you to achieve it."

"It's the possibility of having a dream come true that makes life interesting."

"Everyone seems to have a clear idea of how other people should lead their lives, but none about his or her own."

"Tell your heart that the fear of suffering is worse than the suffering itself."

"When we strive to become better than we are, everything around us becomes better too."

"There is only one way to learn. It's through action."

"If you start by promising what you don't even have yet, you'll lose your desire to work towards getting it."

"People need not fear the unknown if they are capable of achieving what they need and want."

"The secret of life, though, is to fall seven times and to get up eight times."

"We are travelers on a cosmic journey, stardust, swirling and dancing in the eddies and whirlpools of infinity."

Lessons

Follow your dreams: The book emphasizes that everyone has a purpose in life, and it's essential to pursue it no matter the obstacles.

Trust the journey: The journey to your dream may not be easy, and you may face setbacks, but trust the journey and keep going.

Learn from the present: The book encourages people to live in the present and enjoy the journey while striving towards their dreams.

Be open to learning: Every experience offers an opportunity to learn and grow, and it's essential to be open to learning at all times.

Listen to your heart: The book highlights that the heart knows what is truly important, and it's important to listen to your intuition.

Don't be afraid of failure: Failure is an essential part of the journey towards success, and it's essential to embrace it and learn from it.

Believe in yourself: The book emphasizes that we are capable of achieving anything we set our minds to and it's essential to believe in ourselves.

The importance of simplicity: The book teaches us that often, the simplest things in life are the most important, and it's essential to appreciate them.

Pay attention to the signs: The universe gives us signs along the way, and it's essential to pay attention to them and trust the journey.

Embrace change: Change is inevitable, and it's essential to embrace it and adapt to it to move forward in life.

Summary

The Alchemist is a philosophical novel that tells the story of Santiago, a shepherd boy who dreams of a treasure hidden in the Egyptian pyramids. Santiago embarks on a journey to fulfill his dream and encounters various challenges along the way, including bandits, desert storms, and self-doubt.

Throughout his journey, Santiago learns valuable lessons about following his dreams, listening to his heart, and trusting the universe. He meets several characters who help him along the way, including an alchemist who teaches him the principles of the universe and the power of transformation.

In the end, Santiago discovers that the treasure he sought was not material wealth but the realization of his personal legend, the purpose for which he was meant to live. The book emphasizes the importance of pursuing one's dreams, listening to one's heart, and trusting the journey, no matter how challenging it may be. It encourages readers to embrace change and appreciate the simplicity of life while striving towards their dreams.

59. A New Earth: Awakening to Your Life's Purpose by Eckhart Tolle

Quotes

"The primary cause of unhappiness is never the situation but your thoughts about it."

"The past has no power over the present moment."

"The ego is always looking to find something – the next possession, person, or experience – to fulfill you and give you a sense of identity."

"When you no longer believe everything you think, you step out of thought and see clearly that the thinker is not who you are."

"The more consciousness you bring into the body, the stronger the immune system becomes."

"The more you make your thoughts (beliefs, opinions, and judgments) into your identity, the more cut off you are from the spiritual dimension within yourself."

"Awareness is the greatest agent for change."

"To be free of ego is to be free of the fear of nonexistence."

"The more you know yourself, the more clarity there is. Self-knowledge has no end."

"Life is the dancer and you are the dance."

Lessons

The importance of being present in the present moment and not letting past or future worries consume us.

The identification and understanding of the ego as the root of much suffering and the importance of releasing attachment to it.

The concept of the pain-body and how it can manifest in our lives and relationships, and the importance of healing it.

The role of consciousness in shaping our perceptions and creating our reality.

The importance of awareness and mindfulness in every aspect of our lives, including thoughts, emotions, and actions.

The recognition that we are all interconnected and that true happiness and fulfillment can only be found in unity and compassion towards others.

The importance of acceptance and surrender, rather than resistance and control.

The power of silence and stillness in accessing our inner wisdom and connecting with the deeper truths of the universe.

The recognition that life is a journey, and that each moment presents an opportunity for growth and evolution towards our true purpose.

The realization that we are not separate individuals, but rather part of a greater consciousness that transcends the limitations of the ego and the physical world.

Summary

"A New Earth: Awakening to Your Life's Purpose" by Eckhart Tolle is a guidebook to help readers break free from their ego-driven consciousness and awaken to a new level of consciousness that is more connected to the present moment, to others, and to the universe at large. Tolle explores the nature of the ego, the pain-body, and the role of consciousness in shaping our perceptions of reality. He also discusses the importance of mindfulness, acceptance, and surrender, as well as the power of silence and stillness in accessing our inner wisdom. Ultimately, the book aims to help readers realize their life's purpose and to move towards a more fulfilling, harmonious, and compassionate existence. Through his insightful teachings, Tolle invites readers to embark on a journey of self-discovery, transformation, and awakening, leading to a greater sense of inner peace, joy, and fulfillment.

60. The Untethered Soul: The Journey Beyond Yourself by Michael A. Singer

Quotes

"There is nothing more important to true growth than realizing that you are not the voice of the mind - you are the one who hears it."

"The mind is always telling you that you need to change something out there, but the world doesn't need to change. The only thing that needs to change is you."

"The only way to inner freedom is through the one who watches, which is your true self."

"If you truly love someone, your love sees past their humanness. Your love sees their soul."

"The greatest power you have in your life is the power to choose your thoughts."

"To attain true inner freedom, you must be able to objectively watch your problems instead of being lost in them."

"The only reason we don't open our hearts and minds to other people is that they trigger confusion in us that we don't feel brave enough or sane enough to deal with. To the degree that we look clearly and compassionately at ourselves, we feel confident and fearless about looking into someone else's eyes."

"To understand the immeasurable, the mind must be extraordinarily quiet, still."

"If you want to be happy, you have to let go of the part of you that wants to create melodrama. This is the part that thinks there's a reason not to be happy. You have to transcend the personal, and as you do, you will naturally awaken to the higher aspects of your being. In the end, enjoying life's experiences is the only rational thing to do. You're sitting on a planet spinning around in the middle of absolutely nowhere. Go ahead, take a look at reality. You're floating in empty space in a universe that goes on forever. If you have to be here, at least be happy and enjoy the experience."

"The only thing you need to do to be free is to be fully aware of who you are and to investigate the validity of every belief that you hold about yourself."

Lessons

We are not our thoughts or emotions. We are the consciousness that observes them.

To achieve true inner freedom, we must learn to objectively observe our problems and emotions, rather than getting lost in them.

Our true self is the one who observes our thoughts, emotions, and experiences. This self is separate from our ego, which is the aspect of ourselves that seeks validation and control.

By cultivating a practice of mindfulness and meditation, we can learn to quiet our minds and connect with our true selves.

Love is not dependent on external circumstances or the behavior of others. True love comes from within, and it sees past the human limitations of others to connect with their soul.

Happiness is a choice, and we can choose to let go of the thoughts and beliefs that keep us from experiencing joy.

The mind often seeks external validation and control, but true fulfillment comes from connecting with our inner self and letting go of attachment to outcomes.

We are all interconnected, and our actions and thoughts have an impact on others. By cultivating love, compassion, and awareness, we can contribute to a more peaceful and loving world.

All beliefs are ultimately illusions, and by investigating the validity of our beliefs, we can free ourselves from limiting patterns and ideas.

True growth and transformation come from accepting and embracing all aspects of ourselves, including our imperfections and weaknesses. By learning to love and accept ourselves, we can experience greater peace and fulfillment in life.

Summary

"The Untethered Soul: The Journey Beyond Yourself" by Michael A. Singer is a guide to spiritual growth and self-discovery. The book teaches readers to recognize and transcend their ego-driven thoughts and emotions in order to connect with their true selves, which is the consciousness that observes them. Singer explains that the mind often seeks external validation and control, but true fulfillment comes from connecting with our inner self and letting go of attachment to outcomes. The book emphasizes the importance of mindfulness and meditation in achieving inner peace and freedom, as well as the power of love and compassion in creating a more peaceful and loving world. Overall, "The Untethered Soul" provides a practical and insightful guide to living a more conscious, fulfilling life.

CHAPTER 13
Creativity and Innovation
61. Creativity, Inc.: Overcoming the Unseen Forces That Stand in the Way of True Inspiration by Ed Catmull and Amy Wallace

Quotes

"If you give a good idea to a mediocre team, they will screw it up. If you give a mediocre idea to a brilliant team, they will either fix it or throw it away and come up with something better."

"To be a truly creative company, you must start things that might fail."

"The hallmark of a healthy creative culture is that its people feel free to share ideas, opinions, and criticisms."

"It's not the manager's job to prevent risks. It's the manager's job to make it safe for others to take them."

"If you aren't experiencing failure, then you are making a far worse mistake: You are being driven by the desire to avoid it."

"When faced with a challenge, get smarter."

"The best way to predict the future is to invent it."

"It is not the manager's job to solve problems. It is the manager's job to create a culture in which problems can be solved."

"The goal is not to prevent mistakes or failures altogether but to create an environment where we recover quickly and avoid making the same mistake twice."

"If there is more truth in the hallways than in meetings, you have a problem."

Lessons

Embrace failure: Failure is an inevitable part of the creative process. Rather than avoiding it, embrace it and use it as a learning opportunity.

Foster a healthy creative culture: Encourage open communication, a willingness to take risks, and a willingness to challenge assumptions.

Don't fear change: Change is necessary for growth and success. Don't cling to the status quo or be afraid to try new things.

Focus on the team: Build a strong, diverse team that is empowered to make decisions and solve problems.

Trust and respect your colleagues: Trust is essential for creativity to flourish. Create an environment where everyone feels valued and respected.

Stay connected to your audience: It's easy to get lost in the creative process and lose sight of your audience. Continuously seek feedback and strive to understand their needs and desires.

Never stop learning: Stay curious, ask questions, and continuously seek new knowledge and skills.

Build a culture of candor: Encourage honest feedback and don't shy away from tough conversations.

Manage for creativity: Manage for the creative process, not just the end product. Encourage experimentation, collaboration, and innovation.

Create a safe space for creativity: Create an environment where people feel comfortable taking risks, sharing ideas, and being vulnerable.

Summary

Creativity, Inc. is a book that explores the inner workings of Pixar Animation Studios, one of the most successful animation studios in the world. Written by Ed Catmull, one of the co-founders of Pixar, the book offers valuable insights into the creative process and how to overcome the obstacles that can stand in the way of true inspiration.

The book covers a wide range of topics, including the importance of fostering a healthy creative culture, the role of failure in the creative process, the value of diverse perspectives, and the need to stay connected to your audience. Throughout the book, Catmull shares numerous examples from his time at Pixar, including the challenges they faced during the production of movies such as Toy Story, Finding Nemo, and Up.

One of the main takeaways from the book is the importance of building a strong, diverse team that is empowered to make decisions and solve problems. Catmull emphasizes the need to create an environment where people feel comfortable taking risks, sharing ideas, and being vulnerable. He also stresses the importance of staying connected to your audience and continuously seeking feedback.

Overall, Creativity, Inc. is a valuable resource for anyone involved in the creative process, from artists and writers to managers and executives. It offers practical advice and inspiring insights that can help individuals and organizations overcome the unseen forces that can stand in the way of true inspiration.

62. The Artist's Way: A Spiritual Path to Higher Creativity by Julia Cameron

Quotes

"Creativity is God's gift to us. Using our creativity is our gift back to God."

"Leap, and the net will appear."

"The rewards of creativity are greater than the rewards of conformity."

"We are all creative. We all have a secret wish to do something special."

"The capacity for delight is the gift of paying attention."

"The Artist Date is a once-weekly, festive, solo expedition to explore something that interests you."

"As we open our creative channel to the Creator, many gentle but powerful changes are to be expected."

"We learn as we go. We learn as we write. We learn as we paint."

"What we really want to do is what we are really meant to do. When we do what we are meant to do, money comes to us, doors open for us, we feel useful, and the work we do feels like play to us."

"There is no need to go looking for love when it is overflowing within you."

Lessons

Creativity is a natural human trait that everyone possesses, and it's important to cultivate and nurture it.

The creative process is a spiritual journey that requires trust, courage, and a willingness to take risks.

Creative blocks and self-doubt are common obstacles that can be overcome through various techniques, such as morning pages and artist dates.

Negative beliefs about oneself and one's creativity can be transformed through positive affirmations and self-compassion.

Creativity requires discipline and regular practice, but it can also be playful and joyful.

The creative process is not just about producing art or writing, but also about exploring new ideas and discovering one's true self.

Collaboration and support from other creatives can be incredibly helpful and inspiring.

Creativity can lead to a deeper connection with one's spirituality and a greater sense of purpose in life.

Pursuing creative endeavors can lead to personal growth and transformation, as well as new opportunities and abundance.

Embracing one's creativity can lead to a more fulfilling and meaningful life.

Summary

"The Artist's Way" is a book by Julia Cameron that outlines a spiritual path to higher creativity. The book presents a 12-week program designed to help readers overcome creative blocks and cultivate their creativity through a variety of techniques, including morning pages, artist dates, and creative exercises. The author emphasizes the importance of self-discovery and self-compassion, encouraging readers to explore their creativity as a means of connecting with their spirituality and discovering their true selves. Throughout the book, Cameron stresses the idea that everyone is creative and that pursuing creative endeavors can lead to personal growth and transformation, as well as new opportunities and abundance. Overall, "The Artist's Way" is a comprehensive guide to unlocking creativity and living a more fulfilling and meaningful life.

63. The War of Art: Break Through the Blocks and Win Your Inner Creative Battles by Steven Pressfield

Quotes

"Resistance is the most toxic force on the planet. It is the root of more unhappiness than poverty, disease, and erectile dysfunction."

"The more important a call or action is to our soul's evolution, the more Resistance we will feel toward pursuing it."

"Most of us have two lives. The life we live, and the unlived life within us. Between the two stands Resistance."

"The most pernicious aspect of procrastination is that it can become a habit. We don't just put off our lives today; we put them off till our deathbed."

"To labor in the arts for any reason other than love is prostitution."

"The professional has learned that success, like happiness, comes as a by-product of work."

"Creative work is not a selfish act or a bid for attention on the part of the actor. It's a gift to the world and every being in it. Don't cheat us of your contribution. Give us what you've got."

"The artist must be like that marine [solder]. He has to know how to be miserable. He has to love being miserable. He has to take pride in being more miserable than any soldier or swabbie or jet jockey. Because this is war, baby. And war is hell."

"The most important thing about art is to work. Nothing else matters except sitting down every day and trying."

"If you find yourself asking yourself (and your friends), 'Am I really a writer? Am I really an artist?' chances are you are. The counterfeit innovator is wildly self-confident. The real one is scared to death."

Lessons

Resistance is the enemy of creativity and must be recognized and overcome.

The pursuit of creative work requires discipline, consistency, and a professional attitude.

The fear of failure and self-doubt can be powerful obstacles, but they must be confronted and overcome.

The creative process is a constant battle that requires persistence, resilience, and the ability to handle rejection and criticism.

The pursuit of creativity is a noble calling and requires a commitment to making a positive contribution to the world.

True creativity requires the willingness to take risks, make mistakes, and push beyond one's comfort zone.

The pursuit of creative work is a lifelong journey, and there are no shortcuts or easy paths to success.

The act of creating is a transformative experience that can lead to personal growth and fulfillment.

The greatest barrier to creative success is often the self-imposed limitations and beliefs we place on ourselves.

Every creative act is a form of rebellion against the status quo and requires courage, tenacity, and a willingness to challenge conventional wisdom.

Summary

"The War of Art: Break Through the Blocks and Win Your Inner Creative Battles" by Steven Pressfield is a motivational book that explores the concept of resistance, the enemy of creativity. The book provides insight into the inner battles that artists, writers, and other creative professionals face and offers practical advice for overcoming self-doubt, procrastination, and other obstacles that prevent people from realizing their creative potential.

Pressfield argues that creativity is a noble pursuit that requires discipline, consistency, and a professional attitude. The book is divided into three parts: Resistance, Combating Resistance, and Beyond Resistance. In the first part, the author explains the concept of resistance, which he describes as the force that prevents people from doing their best work. He argues that resistance is the root cause of most unhappiness, and that it can be overcome by recognizing it, understanding its sources, and committing to a creative practice.

The second part of the book provides strategies for combating resistance, such as developing a daily routine, setting realistic goals, and learning to embrace failure. The author also discusses the importance of persistence, courage, and resilience in the face of rejection, criticism, and self-doubt.

The final part of the book focuses on the rewards of overcoming resistance and pursuing a creative life. Pressfield argues that creativity is a transformative experience that can lead to personal growth, fulfillment, and a positive contribution to the world.

Overall, "The War of Art" is a powerful and inspiring book that provides valuable insights and practical advice for anyone seeking to break through creative blocks and overcome resistance in their pursuit of a creative life.

64. Steal Like an Artist: 10 Things Nobody Told You About Being Creative by Austin Kleon

Quotes

"Nothing is original. Steal from anywhere that resonates with inspiration or fuels your imagination."

"The only way to find your voice is to use it."

"Don't wait until you know who you are to get started."

"You are, in fact, a mashup of what you choose to let into your life."

"The best way to get started on the path to sharing your work is to think about what you want to learn, and make a commitment to learning it in front of others."

"You're not a genius or a visionary. You're not here to reinvent the wheel. You're here to make a dent in the universe."

"It's one thing to be inspired by others, but it's another to mimic them."

"Don't worry about people stealing your ideas. If your ideas are any good, you'll have to ram them down people's throats."

"Be boring. It's the only way to get work done."

"The most important thing about art is to work. Nothing else matters except sitting down every day and trying."

Lessons

Nothing is completely original, so it's okay to take inspiration from others.

To find your creative voice, you have to start creating.

Don't wait for permission or clarity to start creating. Just start.

Your life experiences and the things you let into your life shape who you are as a creator.

Share your creative work with others and commit to learning and growing.

You don't have to be a genius to create something meaningful.

It's important to be inspired by others without simply copying them.

Don't worry about others stealing your ideas, focus on creating and sharing them.

Consistency and routine are crucial for creative work.

The most important thing about being a creator is to keep creating and putting in the work.

Summary

"Steal Like an Artist" by Austin Kleon is a guidebook for aspiring artists, writers, and creatives looking to develop their skills and find their voice. The book emphasizes that nothing is completely original and encourages readers to take inspiration from the world around them. The author stresses the importance of starting and committing to consistent, daily work. Additionally, the book addresses the fear of sharing one's creative work and offers practical tips for overcoming it. The book's main message is that creativity is a process and that everyone has the ability to create something meaningful. Overall, "Steal Like an Artist" is an inspiring and practical guide for anyone looking to develop their creative skills and overcome creative blocks.

65. Big Magic: Creative Living Beyond Fear by Elizabeth Gilbert

Quotes

"Do whatever brings you to life, then. Follow your own fascinations, obsessions, and compulsions. Trust them. Create whatever causes a revolution in your heart."

"Fear is always triggered by creativity, because creativity asks you to enter into realms of uncertain outcome."

"The universe buries strange jewels deep within us all, and then stands back to see if we can find them."

"Creativity is sacred, and it is not sacred. What we make matters enormously, and it doesn't matter at all."

"Perfection is the death of all good things, the birth of frustration and the mother of procrastination."

"I believe that our planet is inhabited not only by animals and plants and bacteria and viruses, but also by ideas. Ideas are a disembodied, energetic life-form."

"Most things have already been done - but they have not yet been done by you."

"Your fear will always be triggered by your creativity, because creativity asks you to enter into realms of uncertain outcome."

"If you're alive, you're a creative person."

"Done is better than good."

Lessons

"Big Magic: Creative Living Beyond Fear" by Elizabeth Gilbert is a book that offers many valuable lessons for creative people. Here are a few of the key lessons from the book:

Creativity is a mysterious and magical force that can be harnessed by anyone who is willing to take risks and follow their curiosity.

Fear is a natural and necessary part of the creative process, but it should not be allowed to hold you back from exploring your ideas and pursuing your passions.

Inspiration can come from anywhere and at any time, and it is up to you to be open and receptive to the ideas that come your way.

Success and failure are both part of the creative journey, and it is important to embrace both and learn from them.

The creative process is messy and unpredictable, and it is important to be willing to experiment, make mistakes, and try new things.

Collaboration and community are essential for creativity, and it is important to surround yourself with people who support and encourage your creative pursuits.

Creative work requires discipline and dedication, and it is important to show up and do the work even when you don't feel like it.

Comparison and competition can be toxic to creativity, and it is important to focus on your own unique vision and voice.

Creativity is not just about making art, but about living a rich and fulfilling life that is infused with curiosity, wonder, and joy.

The most important thing is to keep creating, even when it is difficult, because the act of creation itself is a powerful and transformative force.

Summary

"Big Magic: Creative Living Beyond Fear" by Elizabeth Gilbert is a book about creativity and the creative process. In the book, Gilbert shares her own experiences as a writer and offers insights and advice for anyone who wants to pursue a creative life.

The book is divided into six sections, each of which explores a different aspect of creativity. In the first section, Gilbert discusses the nature of creativity and how it can be harnessed and nurtured. She emphasizes the importance of curiosity, courage, and persistence in the creative process.

In the second section, Gilbert explores the role of fear in creativity and offers strategies for overcoming fear and self-doubt. She encourages readers to embrace their fears and to use them as a source of creative energy.

In the third section, Gilbert discusses the concept of inspiration and how it can be found and cultivated. She argues that inspiration is not a mystical or divine force, but rather a practical and accessible resource that is available to everyone.

In the fourth section, Gilbert explores the relationship between creativity and success. She emphasizes the importance of focusing on the creative process rather than the outcome, and encourages readers to embrace both success and failure as part of the creative journey.

In the fifth section, Gilbert discusses the importance of discipline and perseverance in creative work. She emphasizes the importance of showing up and doing the work, even when it is difficult or uninspiring.

Finally, in the sixth section, Gilbert explores the idea that creativity is not just about making art, but about living a rich and fulfilling life. She encourages readers to embrace their creativity in all areas of their lives, and to approach the world with a spirit of curiosity, wonder, and joy.

Overall, "Big Magic: Creative Living Beyond Fear" is a thoughtful and inspiring book that offers valuable insights and advice for anyone who wants to pursue a creative life.

CHAPTER 14
Emotional Intelligence
66.   Emotional Intelligence 2.0 by Travis Bradberry and Jean Greaves

Quotes

"Emotional intelligence is your ability to recognize and understand emotions in yourself and others, and your ability to use this awareness to manage your behavior and relationships."

"The higher your EQ, the more successful you'll be in all areas of your life."

"One of the biggest mistakes people make when it comes to emotional intelligence is thinking it's a fixed trait. It's not. EQ is something you can develop and improve with practice."

"To increase your emotional intelligence, you need to be willing to examine your own behavior and beliefs, and make changes where necessary."

"The ability to manage your emotions and remain calm under pressure has a direct link to your performance. TalentSmart has conducted research with more than a million people, and we've found that 90% of top performers are skilled at managing their emotions in times of stress in order to remain calm and in control."

"Empathy is a critical component of emotional intelligence. It allows you to understand the perspectives, needs, and motivations of other people, and to respond in a way that builds trust and rapport."

"Self-awareness is the foundation of emotional intelligence. Without it, you can't accurately understand your own emotions or the impact they have on others."

"Emotional intelligence is not about being overly emotional or letting your feelings run wild. It's about being in control of your emotions and using them in a positive way to achieve your goals."

"Leaders with high emotional intelligence are able to create a positive work environment, build strong relationships with their team members, and inspire their employees to reach their full potential."

"The more you practice emotional intelligence, the more natural it becomes. Eventually, it will become second nature, and you'll find yourself responding to situations in a more emotionally intelligent way without even thinking about it."

Lessons

Emotional intelligence is a crucial skill for success in all areas of life. It involves recognizing and understanding emotions in yourself and others, and using this awareness to manage your behavior and relationships.

Emotional intelligence is not a fixed trait. It can be developed and improved with practice.

Self-awareness is the foundation of emotional intelligence. To increase your emotional intelligence, you must be willing to examine your own behavior and beliefs, and make changes where necessary.

Empathy is a critical component of emotional intelligence. It allows you to understand the perspectives, needs, and motivations of other people, and to respond in a way that builds trust and rapport.

The ability to manage your emotions and remain calm under pressure has a direct link to your performance. High performers are skilled at managing their emotions in times of stress in order to remain calm and in control.

Emotional intelligence is not about being overly emotional or letting your feelings run wild. It's about being in control of your emotions and using them in a positive way to achieve your goals.

Leaders with high emotional intelligence are able to create a positive work environment, build strong relationships with their team members, and inspire their employees to reach their full potential.

To increase your emotional intelligence, you need to practice self-awareness, self-management, social awareness, and relationship management.

Emotional intelligence is a skill that can be developed at any age, and it's never too late to start working on it.

The more you practice emotional intelligence, the more natural it becomes. Eventually, it will become second nature, and you'll find yourself responding to situations in a more emotionally intelligent way without even thinking about it.

Summary

Emotional Intelligence 2.0 is a practical guidebook that focuses on the development of emotional intelligence, which the authors define as the ability to recognize and understand emotions in oneself and others, and to use this awareness to manage behavior and relationships effectively. The book is divided into four sections: self-awareness, self-management, social awareness, and relationship management. Each section provides strategies and techniques for improving emotional intelligence, including self-reflection exercises, tips for managing stress, and strategies for building strong relationships. The authors argue that emotional intelligence is not a fixed trait and can be developed and improved with practice, and that those who have higher levels of emotional intelligence tend to be more successful in all areas of their lives. The book is full of real-life examples, research findings, and practical tips for readers to improve their emotional intelligence and achieve greater success in their personal and professional lives.

67. The Emotional Intelligence Quick Book by Travis Bradberry and Jean Greaves

Quotes

"Emotional intelligence is the ability to recognize and understand emotions in yourself and others, and your ability to use this awareness to manage your behavior and relationships."

"Emotions are a critical aspect of our lives, influencing everything from our personal relationships to our professional success."

"Emotional intelligence is not fixed – it can be developed and improved through focused effort and practice."

"People with high emotional intelligence are able to control their emotions, stay calm and focused under pressure, and communicate effectively with others."

"Empathy is a key component of emotional intelligence, allowing us to understand and connect with others on a deeper level."

"Self-awareness is the foundation of emotional intelligence, as it allows us to recognize our own emotions and how they impact our thoughts and actions."

"People with high emotional intelligence are able to recognize and manage their own emotions, as well as understand and respond to the emotions of others."

"Emotional intelligence is not just a 'soft skill' – it has real-world impact on our personal and professional success."

"The ability to manage emotions effectively is a key component of emotional intelligence, as it allows us to navigate challenging situations with grace and poise."

"By developing our emotional intelligence, we can improve our relationships, enhance our communication skills, and achieve greater success in all areas of our lives."

Lessons

Emotional intelligence is a crucial aspect of success: Emotional intelligence is not just a "nice-to-have" skill, but a critical one for success in all areas of life, including personal relationships, career, and overall well-being.

Self-awareness is the foundation of emotional intelligence: Self-awareness is the ability to recognize and understand our own emotions, thoughts, and behaviors. It is the foundation upon which emotional intelligence is built.

Emotions can be managed: Emotions are not fixed and uncontrollable. We have the ability to recognize and manage our emotions, as well as understand and respond to the emotions of others.

Empathy is key: Empathy is the ability to understand and share the feelings of others. It is a crucial component of emotional intelligence and allows us to connect with others on a deeper level.

Emotional intelligence can be developed: Emotional intelligence is not fixed or innate; it can be developed and improved through focused effort and practice.

Communication skills are critical: Effective communication is a crucial component of emotional intelligence. Developing strong communication skills can help us to build better relationships and achieve greater success in all areas of life.

Emotional intelligence is not just a "soft skill": Emotional intelligence has real-world impact on our personal and professional success. It can help us to navigate challenging situations with greater ease, build better relationships, and achieve our goals.

Emotional intelligence is a lifelong journey: Developing emotional intelligence is not a one-time achievement, but a lifelong journey of self-awareness, self-improvement, and continuous learning.

Summary

"The Emotional Intelligence Quick Book" by Travis Bradberry and Jean Greaves is a practical guide to understanding and improving emotional intelligence. The book emphasizes that emotional intelligence is a crucial aspect of success in all areas of life, and provides practical strategies for developing emotional intelligence. The book covers topics such as self-awareness, empathy, managing emotions, effective communication, and the real-world impact of emotional intelligence. The authors stress that emotional intelligence is not a fixed or innate trait, but rather something that can be developed and improved through focused effort and practice. Overall, the book provides readers with a practical framework for understanding and developing emotional intelligence, and offers insights and strategies that can be applied in both personal and professional contexts.

68. The Language of Emotional Intelligence: The Five Essential Tools for Building Powerful and Effective Relationships by Jeanne Segal

Quotes

"Emotional intelligence is the ability to understand and manage your own emotions, and to recognize and influence the emotions of others."

"Self-awareness is the foundation of emotional intelligence. Without self-awareness, it's impossible to understand how your emotions and behavior affect others."

"Empathy is the ability to understand and share the feelings of others. It's a critical component of emotional intelligence, and it's essential for building strong, positive relationships."

"Effective communication is key to building strong relationships. It involves not only speaking clearly and directly, but also listening actively and empathetically."

"Conflict is a natural part of relationships, but it can also be an opportunity for growth and understanding. Emotional intelligence can help you manage conflict in a positive and productive way."

"Resilience is the ability to bounce back from adversity and to adapt to changing circumstances. It's an important aspect of emotional intelligence, and it can help you navigate the ups and downs of life with greater ease and grace."

"Cultivating emotional intelligence takes time and practice, but the benefits are worth it. By developing your emotional intelligence, you can build stronger, more meaningful relationships, and live a happier, more fulfilling life."

Lessons

Powerful and Effective Relationships by Jeanne Segal

Self-awareness is essential for developing emotional intelligence. By understanding your own emotions and behaviors, you can better understand and manage your relationships with others.

Empathy is a crucial component of emotional intelligence. By putting yourself in someone else's shoes, you can better understand their perspective and build stronger, more positive relationships.

Effective communication is key to building strong relationships. This involves not only speaking clearly and directly but also listening actively and empathetically.

Conflict is a natural part of relationships, but it can also be an opportunity for growth and understanding. Emotional intelligence can help you manage conflict in a positive and productive way.

Resilience is an important aspect of emotional intelligence. By cultivating resilience, you can bounce back from adversity and adapt to changing circumstances with greater ease and grace.

Cultivating emotional intelligence takes time and practice, but the benefits are worth it. By developing your emotional intelligence, you can build stronger, more meaningful relationships, and live a happier, more fulfilling life.

Emotional intelligence is not just about managing your own emotions, but also about recognizing and influencing the emotions of others. By being aware of the emotions of those around you, you can build stronger relationships and create a more positive environment for everyone.

Summary

The Language of Emotional Intelligence is a book that provides insights into the five essential tools for building powerful and effective relationships. The author, Jeanne Segal, emphasizes that emotional intelligence is a critical aspect of building strong relationships, and it involves understanding and managing your own emotions, as well as recognizing and influencing the emotions of others.

The five essential tools for building emotional intelligence are self-awareness, empathy, effective communication, conflict management, and resilience. The book provides practical strategies and techniques for developing these tools and applying them in real-life situations.

Self-awareness is the foundation of emotional intelligence, and it involves understanding your own emotions and behavior. Empathy is the ability to understand and share the feelings of others, and it is essential for building positive relationships. Effective communication involves both speaking and listening skills, and it is key to building strong relationships.

Conflict is a natural part of relationships, but emotional intelligence can help manage it in a positive and productive way. Resilience is the ability to bounce back from adversity and adapt to changing circumstances, and it is an important aspect of emotional intelligence.

Overall, The Language of Emotional Intelligence is a valuable resource for anyone seeking to develop their emotional intelligence and build stronger, more meaningful relationships. The book provides practical guidance and exercises to help readers develop these essential tools and apply them in their personal and professional lives.

69. The EQ Difference: A Powerful Plan for Putting Emotional Intelligence to Work by Adele B. Lynn

Quotes

"Emotional intelligence is about being aware of and managing your own emotions, as well as recognizing and responding effectively to the emotions of others."

"Emotional intelligence is not about being 'nice' or 'likable', but rather about being authentic and skillful in navigating interpersonal dynamics."

"Emotional intelligence can be developed and improved through intentional practice and self-reflection."

"A key component of emotional intelligence is empathy, which involves putting oneself in another person's shoes and understanding their perspective."

"Effective communication is a critical skill for those with high emotional intelligence, as it allows them to express their own emotions and needs clearly, while also listening actively and responding empathetically to others."

"Leaders who possess high emotional intelligence are often better able to motivate and inspire their teams, build strong relationships with colleagues and customers, and navigate conflicts and challenges with grace and skill."

"To develop greater emotional intelligence, it is important to cultivate self-awareness, practice self-regulation, develop empathy and social skills, and work to build positive relationships with others."

Lessons

Emotional intelligence (EQ) is a critical skill for success in the workplace and in life. EQ involves being aware of and managing your own emotions, as well as recognizing and responding effectively to the emotions of others.

EQ can be developed and improved through intentional practice and self-reflection. By focusing on improving your self-awareness, self-regulation, empathy, and social skills, you can become more emotionally intelligent and better able to navigate interpersonal dynamics.

One of the key components of EQ is empathy, which involves putting yourself in another person's shoes and understanding their perspective. By practicing empathy, you can build stronger relationships with others and better navigate conflicts and challenges.

Effective communication is a critical skill for those with high EQ. By expressing your own emotions and needs clearly, while also listening actively and responding empathetically to others, you can build strong relationships and navigate interpersonal dynamics with greater ease.

Leaders who possess high EQ are often better able to motivate and inspire their teams, build strong relationships with colleagues and customers, and navigate conflicts and challenges with grace and skill. By developing your EQ, you can become a more effective and successful leader.

To develop greater emotional intelligence, it is important to cultivate self-awareness, practice self-regulation, develop empathy and social skills, and work to build positive relationships with others. By focusing on these areas, you can improve your EQ and achieve greater success in your personal and professional life.

Summary

The EQ Difference: A Powerful Plan for Putting Emotional Intelligence to Work by Adele B. Lyn is a book that explains the importance of emotional intelligence (EQ) in the workplace and in life, and provides a step-by-step plan for developing greater emotional intelligence. The book highlights the key components of EQ, including self-awareness, self-regulation, empathy, and social skills, and provides practical strategies for developing each of these areas. The book also discusses the benefits of developing EQ, such as improved communication, stronger relationships, and greater success as a leader. Overall, the book provides a comprehensive guide for improving EQ and achieving greater success in both personal and professional life.

70. The Emotionally Intelligent Manager: How to Develop and Use the Four Key Emotional Skills of Leadership by David R. Caruso and Peter Salovey

Quotes

"Emotions drive people, and people drive performance."

"Emotionally intelligent managers are adept at reading the emotional states of others."

"Self-awareness is the foundation of emotional intelligence."

"Emotional intelligence means being able to read and regulate your own emotions and the emotions of others."

"Emotionally intelligent managers know how to use emotions to facilitate better decision making."

"Emotionally intelligent managers create a climate of trust and psychological safety where employees feel free to express themselves."

"Emotional intelligence is not about suppressing emotions, but rather about using them wisely and effectively."

"Emotionally intelligent managers are able to empathize with others and understand their perspectives."

"Effective communication is a key skill for emotionally intelligent managers."

"Emotionally intelligent managers know how to manage their own emotions and keep their cool under pressure."

Lessons

Emotionally intelligent managers are aware of their own emotions, strengths, and weaknesses.

Emotionally intelligent managers are adept at reading the emotional states of others. They understand the emotions of their employees and use this understanding to communicate effectively and build strong relationships.

Emotionally intelligent managers use emotions to facilitate better decision-making. They understand how emotions can influence the decision-making process and use this knowledge to make more effective decisions.

Emotionally intelligent managers create a climate of trust and psychological safety where employees feel free to express themselves. They create an environment where employees feel comfortable sharing their ideas and concerns without fear of retribution.

Effective communication is a key skill for emotionally intelligent managers. They are able to communicate clearly and effectively, and they listen actively to their employees.

Emotionally intelligent managers are able to empathize with others and understand their perspectives. They are able to put themselves in their employees' shoes and see things from their point of view.

Emotionally intelligent managers know how to manage their own emotions and keep their cool under pressure. They are able to regulate their emotions and remain calm in challenging situations.

Emotionally intelligent managers are skilled at giving feedback. They give feedback in a constructive and helpful way, focusing on the behavior rather than the person.

Emotionally intelligent managers understand the importance of work-life balance. They recognize that their employees have lives outside of work and they strive to create a balance between work and personal life.

Emotionally intelligent managers are lifelong learners. They are open to new ideas and approaches and are constantly seeking to improve themselves and their leadership skills.

Summary

The Emotionally Intelligent Manager by David R. Caruso and Peter Salovey is a guide for leaders who want to develop their emotional intelligence skills. The book provides an overview of the four key emotional skills that are essential for effective leadership: self-awareness, self-regulation, motivation, and empathy. It also discusses the importance of effective communication, building trust and psychological safety, managing emotions under pressure, giving feedback, and promoting work-life balance. The authors provide real-life examples and practical advice for developing these skills, and offer tools and strategies for building emotional intelligence. The book is a valuable resource for managers and leaders who want to improve their leadership abilities and create a more positive and productive work environment.

CHAPTER 15

Personal Finance

71. Total Money Makeover: A Proven Plan for Financial Fitness by Dave Ramsey

Quotes

"If you will live like no one else, later you can live like no one else."

"Debt is not a tool. It is a method to make banks rich, not you."

"The only way to change your financial future is to change your financial behavior today."

"If you want to be rich, you have to live like you're broke."

"Personal finance is 80% behavior and only 20% head knowledge. It's what you do, not what you say, that determines your financial fitness."

"The enemy of "the best" is not "the worst." The enemy of "the best" is "just fine.""

"You must gain control over your money or the lack of it will forever control you."

"The borrower is slave to the lender."

"It's not the money that changes people, it's the lack of money that changes people."

"You must walk to the beat of a different drummer. The same beat that the wealthy hear. If the beat sounds normal, evacuate the dance floor immediately! The goal is to not be normal, because as my radio listeners know, normal is broke."

Lessons

Start by creating a budget: Creating a budget is an important step towards achieving financial fitness. By creating a budget, you can track your spending and identify areas where you can cut back to save money.

Get rid of debt: Debt is one of the biggest obstacles to financial freedom. The book emphasizes on the importance of eliminating debt by adopting a debt snowball approach, where you pay off the smallest debt first and then move on to the next one.

Save for emergencies: It is important to have an emergency fund that can cover your expenses for at least three to six months. This can help you avoid getting into debt in case of an unexpected event such as job loss or medical emergency.

Invest for the future: The book encourages readers to start investing early for their future, whether it is for retirement or other long-term goals. The author suggests mutual funds as a good option for those who are new to investing.

Live below your means: The book stresses on the importance of living below your means, by cutting down on unnecessary expenses and avoiding lifestyle inflation. This can help you save more and achieve financial freedom sooner.

Be disciplined and patient: The book emphasizes on the importance of being disciplined and patient when it comes to achieving financial fitness. It is not a quick fix, but rather a journey that requires commitment and perseverance.

Give generously: The book encourages readers to give generously, whether it is to charity or to help someone in need. This can bring a sense of purpose and fulfillment to your life.

Summary

The book Total Money Makeover: A Proven Plan for Financial Fitness by Dave Ramsey provides a step-by-step plan to achieve financial freedom. The book emphasizes on the importance of creating a budget, getting rid of debt, saving for emergencies, investing for the future, living below your means, being disciplined and patient, and giving generously. The author advocates a debt snowball approach, where you pay off your smallest debt first and then move on to the next one. The book also stresses on the importance of living a simple lifestyle and avoiding unnecessary expenses to save more. Overall, the book provides practical and actionable advice to achieve financial fitness and build wealth.

72. Your Money or Your Life by Vicki Robin and Joe Dominguez

Quotes

"Money is something we choose to trade our life energy for."

"We live in a culture that has been hijacked by the promise of more."

"We don't inherit the earth from our ancestors, we borrow it from our children."

"The only way to save money is to not spend it."

"The goal is to have enough, not to have more."

"The best things in life are free, but some of the most important things require money."

"Money can buy you happiness, but only up to a certain point."

"We are not our possessions, our job titles, or our bank accounts."

"The more we have, the more we have to lose."

"The real riches in life come from the relationships we have with others and the experiences we share."

Lessons

Shift your perspective on money: Money is a representation of your life energy and time, and it's important to understand the true value of what you're trading it for.

Track your spending: Keep track of all your expenses to gain a clear understanding of where your money is going and how you can cut back.

Embrace frugality: Frugality doesn't mean deprivation; it means finding joy in the simple things in life and being intentional with your spending.

Invest in yourself: Investing in your own education and personal growth is the best investment you can make.

Prioritize financial independence: Achieving financial independence means having enough savings and investments to cover your living expenses without relying on a job or other sources of income.

Seek fulfillment beyond material possessions: Happiness and fulfillment come from experiences, relationships, and personal growth, not from accumulating more stuff.

Make conscious spending choices: Before making a purchase, consider its true value and whether it aligns with your values and goals.

Focus on the big picture: Financial freedom and fulfillment come from focusing on the big picture of your life, not just the day-to-day minutiae.

Take responsibility for your financial life: You have the power to take control of your financial situation and create a better future for yourself.

Use money as a tool for positive change: Your money can be used to support causes and organizations you believe in and make a positive impact on the world around you.

Summary

"Your Money or Your Life" by Vicki Robin and Joe Dominguez is a personal finance book that emphasizes the importance of understanding the true value of money and the role it plays in our lives. The book argues that money is a representation of our life energy, and we should be intentional about how we spend it. The authors offer practical advice on how to track expenses, reduce unnecessary spending, and invest in personal growth to achieve financial independence. The book also encourages readers to prioritize experiences, relationships, and personal fulfillment over material possessions. By taking responsibility for our financial lives and making conscious spending choices, we can create a better future for ourselves and positively impact the world around us. Overall, "Your Money or Your Life" provides a holistic approach to personal finance and encourages readers to view money as a tool for positive change.

73. The Richest Man in Babylon by George S. Clason

Quotes

"The more of wisdom we know, the more we may earn. That man who seeks to learn more of his craft shall be richly rewarded."

"A part of all you earn is yours to keep. It should be not less than a tenth no matter how little you earn. It can be as much more as you can afford."

"The soul of a free man looks at life as a series of problems to be solved and solves them, while the soul of a slave whines, 'What can I do who am but a slave?'"

"Opportunity is a haughty goddess who wastes no time with those who are unprepared."

"The only way to become wealthy is to save a portion of your income, no matter how small, and to put it into a safe, secure investment."

"Wealth that comes quickly disappears quickly, but wealth that is built slowly lasts a lifetime."

"Money is plentiful for those who understand the simple laws which govern its acquisition."

"A man's wealth is not in the coins he carries in his purse; it is in the income he builds, the golden stream that continually flows into his purse and keeps it always bulging."

"Better a little caution than a great regret."

"The first step towards riches is desire. The second step is faith."

Lessons

Save a portion of your income: One of the key lessons of the book is the importance of saving a portion of your income, no matter how small it may be. The book recommends saving at least 10% of your income, and putting it into a safe, secure investment.

Invest wisely: The book stresses the importance of investing wisely, and warns against speculation and taking unnecessary risks. The book recommends investing in assets that have a proven track record of growth and stability.

Seek advice from knowledgeable people: The book emphasizes the importance of seeking advice from people who are knowledgeable and experienced in financial matters. This can include financial advisors, bankers, and successful business people.

Live below your means: The book stresses the importance of living below your means, and avoiding unnecessary expenses. By living frugally, you can save more money and invest it wisely.

Work hard and be disciplined: The book emphasizes the importance of hard work and discipline in achieving financial success. It encourages readers to be persistent in their efforts, and to maintain a disciplined approach to money management.

Have a plan: The book stresses the importance of having a financial plan and sticking to it. This can involve setting goals, creating a budget, and regularly reviewing your progress.

Take calculated risks: The book encourages readers to take calculated risks, but warns against speculation and unnecessary risk-taking. By carefully weighing the risks and potential rewards of an investment, you can make informed decisions and increase your chances of success.

Be patient: The book emphasizes the importance of patience in achieving financial success. It reminds readers that wealth is built slowly over time, and that there are no shortcuts to success.

Avoid debt: The book warns against taking on excessive debt, and emphasizes the importance of living within your means. By avoiding debt and living frugally, you can save more money and invest it wisely.

Give back: The book encourages readers to give back to their communities and to help others who are less fortunate. It reminds readers that true wealth is not just about accumulating money, but also about making a positive impact on the world around us.

Summary

The Richest Man in Babylon by George S. Clason is a book that provides practical advice on personal finance and wealth building through a series of parables set in ancient Babylon. The book is structured around a series of financial lessons, each of which is illustrated through the experiences of various characters in Babylon.

The book emphasizes the importance of saving a portion of your income, investing wisely, seeking advice from knowledgeable people, living below your means, working hard and being disciplined, having a plan, taking calculated risks, being patient, avoiding debt, and giving back to your community.

Through its parables, the book stresses the timeless principles of sound money management and provides readers with practical advice on how to build wealth over time. The book is written in an accessible and engaging style, making it a valuable resource for anyone who wants to improve their financial situation and achieve greater financial security.

74. The Bogleheads' Guide to Investing by Taylor Larimore, Mel Lindauer, and Michael LeBoeuf

Quotes

"In investing, you get what you don't pay for. Costs matter. So intelligent investors will use low-cost index funds to build a diversified portfolio of stocks and bonds, and they will stay the course."

"The stock market is a giant distraction to the business of investing. The market serves as a public opinion poll and nothing more."

"The single greatest enemy of successful investing is Wall Street itself."

"The more you trade, the less you keep."

"The true cost of investing lies not in the expense ratio, but in the returns you give up by settling for inferior long-term performance."

"Diversification is the only free lunch in investing."

"If you don't understand it, don't invest in it."

"It's not how much money you make that will determine your future prosperity. It's how much you keep."

"The four most dangerous words in investing are: 'This time it's different.'"

"The market always fluctuates, but the beauty of low-cost indexing is that it allows you to capture the good times and survive the bad times."

Lessons

Keep costs low: One of the key lessons from the book is the importance of keeping investment costs low. This can be achieved through investing in low-cost index funds, which offer a diversified portfolio with minimal fees.

Avoid market timing: Attempting to time the market or predict future movements is unlikely to lead to successful investing. Instead, investors should focus on building a diversified portfolio and holding it for the long-term.

Stay the course: Another important lesson is to stay the course and resist the urge to make changes to your portfolio based on short-term market movements or other external factors.

Diversify: Diversification is a crucial aspect of investing, as it helps to spread risk across a range of different assets. This can be achieved through investing in index funds that track broad market indices.

Understand what you're investing in: Before investing in any asset, it's important to understand how it works and what factors can affect its performance. Investors should also be aware of any fees or charges associated with their investments.

Focus on the long-term: Successful investing requires a long-term perspective, as short-term fluctuations and market noise can be distracting and lead to poor decision-making. Investors should focus on their long-term goals and develop a disciplined approach to investing.

Keep emotions in check: Emotions can be a major obstacle to successful investing, as they can lead to impulsive decisions and irrational behavior. Investors should learn to keep their emotions in check and avoid making decisions based on fear, greed, or other emotional factors.

Summary

The Bogleheads' Guide to Investing is a comprehensive guide to investing based on the principles of John Bogle, the founder of the Vanguard Group and creator of the first index fund. The book provides practical advice on how to build a diversified portfolio using low-cost index funds, and offers strategies for avoiding common pitfalls such as market timing, excessive trading, and emotional decision-making.

The authors emphasize the importance of keeping investment costs low, staying the course with a long-term perspective, and maintaining a disciplined approach to investing. They also stress the benefits of diversification, and encourage investors to understand what they are investing in and to keep their emotions in check.

Overall, the book provides a clear and accessible introduction to investing, and offers practical advice for both novice and experienced investors looking to build a successful investment portfolio. The Bogleheads' Guide to Investing is a must-read for anyone interested in achieving long-term financial success through disciplined, low-cost investing.

75. The Little Book of Common Sense Investing by John C. Bogle

Quotes

"In investing, you get what you don't pay for."

"Don't look for the needle in the haystack. Just buy the haystack!"

"The more the managers and brokers take, the less investors make."

"Time is your friend; impulse is your enemy."

"Successful investing is about managing risk, not avoiding it."

"The stock market is a giant distraction from the business of investing."

"Don't let emotions cloud your judgment."

"The most important investment decision you can make is not which stocks or mutual funds to buy, but rather, how much of your assets should be in equities and how much in fixed-income investments."

"Investing is not nearly as difficult as it looks. Successful investing involves doing a few things right and avoiding serious mistakes."

"The winning formula for success in investing is owning the entire stock market through an index fund, and then doing nothing."

Lessons

Keep costs low: One of the primary lessons from the book is the importance of keeping investment costs low. Bogle emphasizes that fees and expenses can eat into investment returns, and that investors should seek out low-cost index funds to minimize these expenses.

Avoid market timing: Bogle cautions against trying to time the market, and instead advocates for a buy-and-hold approach. He argues that investors who try to time the market often end up selling low and buying high, which hurts their returns over the long run.

Diversify broadly: Bogle recommends that investors diversify their portfolios across a range of asset classes and geographic regions. By owning a broad range of stocks and bonds, investors can reduce their exposure to any one company or market.

Focus on the long term: Bogle emphasizes the importance of taking a long-term view when it comes to investing. He argues that short-term market fluctuations are noise, and that investors should focus on the fundamentals of the companies they own.

Don't be swayed by emotions: Bogle cautions against making investment decisions based on emotions. He advises investors to stick to a disciplined investment plan and avoid making impulsive decisions based on market news or trends.

Stay the course: Finally, Bogle stresses the importance of staying the course, even in the face of market volatility or short-term setbacks. He argues that investors who stay invested and maintain a long-term perspective are more likely to achieve their financial goals over time.

Summary

The Little Book of Common Sense Investing by John C. Bogle is a concise and practical guide to investing that emphasizes the importance of keeping investment costs low, diversifying broadly, and focusing on the long-term fundamentals of the companies in which one invests. Bogle argues that investors who try to time the market or pick individual stocks are likely to underperform the market over the long run, and that the best way to achieve consistent, long-term returns is to invest in low-cost index funds that track the overall market. He also stresses the importance of avoiding emotional decision-making and sticking to a disciplined investment plan, even in the face of short-term market volatility or setbacks. Overall, the book offers a common-sense approach to investing that is accessible to readers of all levels of experience and expertise.

CHAPTER 16

Decision-Making and Problem-Solving

76. Blink: The Power of Thinking Without Thinking by Malcolm Gladwell

Quotes

"The key to good decision-making is not knowledge. It is understanding. We are swimming in the former. We are desperately lacking in the latter."

"We thin-slice because we have to, and we come to rely on that ability because there are lots of situations where careful attention to the details of a very thin slice, even for no more than a second or two, can tell us an awful lot."

"Insight is not a lightbulb that goes off inside our heads. It is a flickering candle that can easily be snuffed out."

"The first task of Blink is to convince you of a simple fact: decisions made very quickly can be every bit as good as decisions made cautiously and deliberately."

"Our world requires that decisions be sourced and footnoted, and if we say how we feel, we must also be prepared to elaborate on why we feel that way...We need to respect the fact that it is possible to know without knowing why we know and accept that - sometimes - we're better off that way."

"The key to good decision making is not knowledge. It is understanding. We are swimming in the former. We are desperately lacking in the latter."

"Truly successful decision-making relies on a balance between deliberate and instinctive thinking."

"The task of making sense of ourselves and our behavior requires that we acknowledge there can be as much value in the blink of an eye as in months of rational analysis."

"We have, as human beings, a storytelling problem. We're a bit too quick to come up with explanations for things we don't really have an explanation for."

"We live in a world that assumes that the quality of a decision is directly related to the time and effort that went into making it."

Lessons

Our initial judgments and first impressions can be just as accurate as decisions made after careful consideration and analysis.

The unconscious mind plays a significant role in decision-making, and sometimes it can be more reliable than conscious thought.

We can improve our decision-making by honing our ability to recognize and trust our intuition.

We should be aware of our biases and work to minimize their influence on our decisions.

We should strive for a balance between quick, intuitive decision-making and deliberate, analytical decision-making.

Sometimes, too much information can actually hinder our ability to make good decisions.

Rapid cognition, or the ability to make quick decisions based on limited information, can be developed and improved through practice and experience.

Our emotions and past experiences can impact our intuition and decision-making, and we should be aware of how they influence our choices.

Nonverbal communication, such as body language and facial expressions, can provide important information that can be used in decision-making.

We should be open to the idea that there are situations in which we can trust our instincts and make decisions quickly and confidently, without needing to analyze every detail.

Summary

In his book "Blink: The Power of Thinking Without Thinking," Malcolm Gladwell explores the power of intuition and quick decision-making. He argues that in certain situations, we can make accurate decisions very quickly, relying on our unconscious mind to process information and guide us towards the right choice.

Gladwell presents numerous examples to support this idea, from the ability of art experts to instantly recognize a fake painting, to the success of professional tennis players who are able to make split-second decisions about where to hit the ball.

He also discusses the role that our past experiences, emotions, and biases can play in our decision-making process, and suggests ways to recognize and overcome these influences.

Overall, the book challenges the notion that more information and analysis always leads to better decision-making, and encourages readers to trust their instincts and develop their ability to make quick, intuitive decisions when appropriate.

77. Decisive: How to Make Better Choices in Life and Work by Chip Heath and Dan Heath

Quotes

"When we encounter a decision, we should not ask ourselves 'What do I want?' Instead we should ask 'What are my options?'"

"The hardest thing about a decision is that you don't know if it's right or wrong until after you've made it."

"We should all aspire to be the captain of our own ship, but we also need to acknowledge that sometimes we're adrift and in need of help."

"We can't make perfect decisions, but we can make better ones."

"Narrow framing is the tendency to define our choices too narrowly, to see them in binary terms, and to overlook creative solutions."

"Reality is a cloud of possibility, not a point. The more we scrutinize that cloud, the more we understand how many opportunities we have."

"A decision is only as good as the process that produced it."

"It's natural to seek out confirming information, but it's essential to also seek out disconfirming information."

"The more options we have, the more likely we are to make a good decision."

"We often overestimate the importance of the decision itself, and underestimate the importance of the process."

Lessons

Expand your options: Don't limit yourself to a few obvious choices, consider multiple alternatives and explore creative solutions.

Reality test your assumptions: Challenge your assumptions and consider the evidence that might disprove your preferred choice.

Attain distance before deciding: Take a step back and gain perspective before making a decision. Consider the long-term consequences of your decision.

Prepare to be wrong: Be open to the possibility that your decision may be wrong, and have a backup plan in place.

Avoid narrow framing: Avoid defining choices too narrowly, and seek out a broader range of options.

Take action: Once you have made a decision, take action and commit to it. Don't let indecision or analysis paralysis hold you back.

Learn from your experiences: Reflect on your past decisions and learn from your successes and failures. Use this knowledge to inform your future decisions.

Seek out diverse perspectives: Don't rely solely on your own viewpoint. Seek out diverse perspectives and listen to the opinions of others.

Manage your emotions: Emotions can cloud your judgment and lead to poor decision-making. Learn to manage your emotions and make decisions based on rational thinking.

Improve your decision-making process: A good decision is only as good as the process that produced it. Continuously refine and improve your decision-making process.

Summary

"Decisive: How to Make Better Choices in Life and Work" by Chip Heath and Dan Heath is a practical guide for improving decision-making. The authors argue that many common decision-making pitfalls can be avoided by following a four-step process: Widen your options, reality-test your assumptions, attain distance before deciding, and prepare to be wrong. They also emphasize the importance of avoiding narrow framing, seeking out diverse perspectives, managing emotions, and continuously improving the decision-making process. The book draws on a wide range of examples and research, and provides numerous strategies and tools for making better decisions in both personal and professional contexts. Overall, the book offers a valuable framework for improving decision-making skills that can be applied in a variety of situations.

78. The Checklist Manifesto: How to Get Things Right by Atul Gawande

Quotes

"The volume and complexity of what we know has exceeded our individual ability to deliver its benefits correctly, safely, or reliably. Knowledge has both saved us and burdened us."

"The problem is not ignorance, but rather the illusion of knowledge."

"Under conditions of complexity, not only are checklists a help, they are required for success."

"Checklists remind us of the minimum necessary steps and make them explicit. They not only offer the possibility of verification but also instill a kind of discipline of higher performance."

"The power of checklists is limited, however, by the fact that success hinges on their consistent use."

"The most profound thing about checklists is their ability to create a culture of teamwork and discipline."

"Good checklists, on the other hand are precise. They are efficient, to the point, and easy to use even in the most difficult situations."

"In medicine, we rely on people to remember everything—to have knowledge, to have a good memory, to be diligent, and to have a kind of moral commitment to the right thing. The problem is that the volume and complexity of what we know has exceeded our individual ability to deliver its benefits correctly, safely, or reliably."

"The checklist gets the dumb stuff out of the way, the routines your brain shouldn't have to occupy itself with (Are the elevator controls set? Did the patient get her antibiotics on time?), and lets it rise above to focus on the hard stuff (Where should we place the incision?).

"We don't like checklists. They can be painstaking. They're not much fun. But I don't think the issue here is mere laziness. There's something deeper, more visceral going on when people walk away not only from saving lives but from making money. It somehow feels beneath us to use a checklist, an embarrassment. It runs counter to deeply held beliefs about how the truly great among us—those we aspire to be—handle situations of high stakes and complexity. The truly great are daring. They improvise. They do not have protocols and checklists. Maybe our idea of heroism needs updating."

Lessons

Checklists can help prevent errors and improve outcomes in complex tasks.

Checklists can help ensure consistency in high-stress, high-stakes situations.

Good checklists are precise, efficient, and easy to use, even in difficult situations.

Checklists can create a culture of teamwork and discipline.

The power of checklists is limited by their consistent use.

The volume and complexity of knowledge today have exceeded our individual ability to deliver its benefits correctly, safely, or reliably.

Ignorance is not the problem; it is the illusion of knowledge.

Using checklists can free up mental space and allow us to focus on more complex tasks.

We need to update our ideas of heroism and recognize that using checklists is not a sign of weakness but a way to achieve excellence.

Checklists are not just for routine tasks but can be valuable in any complex, high-stakes situation, including surgery, aviation, and construction.

Summary

The Checklist Manifesto by Atul Gawande argues that checklists can help improve outcomes in complex tasks and high-stress situations. The book examines how checklists are used in various fields, including medicine, aviation, and construction, and how they can be designed to be precise, efficient, and easy to use. Gawande also explores the cultural and psychological barriers to using checklists and the benefits of overcoming them, including creating a culture of teamwork and discipline. Overall, the book emphasizes the importance of using checklists to prevent errors and achieve excellence in any complex, high-stakes situation.

79. Black Box Thinking: Why Most People Never Learn from Their Mistakes - But Some Do by Matthew Syed

Quotes

"The most successful individuals, teams, and organizations are those that are constantly learning, constantly experimenting, and constantly pushing themselves to be better than they were yesterday."

"The willingness to learn from failure is the secret to success."

"The greatest obstacle to progress and innovation is not ignorance but the illusion of knowledge."

"The key to success is not avoiding failure but learning from it."

"The most successful people are not those who never fail, but those who learn from their failures and use that knowledge to improve."

"We must embrace failure and make it our friend, not our enemy."

"If you're not failing, you're not pushing your limits, and if you're not pushing your limits, you're not maximizing your potential."

"The only way to truly fail is to give up and stop trying."

"Success is not a destination, it is a journey, and the only way to keep moving forward on that journey is to keep learning from our mistakes."

"The key to success is not perfection, but resilience in the face of failure."

Lessons

Practice Reflection: Reflection is key to learning from mistakes. To improve, you must be able to analyze what went wrong, why it went wrong, and how you can prevent it from happening again.

Adopt a Growth Mindset: A growth mindset means understanding that skills and abilities can be developed and improved over time, rather than being fixed traits. This allows you to be more resilient in the face of failure and to view mistakes as opportunities to learn.

Encourage Openness: Organizations that encourage openness and transparency are more likely to learn from their mistakes. This means creating an environment where people feel comfortable admitting when they have made a mistake, and where mistakes are seen as opportunities to learn and improve.

Experiment and Innovate: Innovation requires experimentation, which in turn requires a willingness to take risks and the acceptance that failure is a natural part of the process. Organizations that are willing to take risks and experiment are more likely to find new and better ways of doing things.

Learn from Other Fields: Many industries can learn from the way others approach failure. For example, the aviation industry has developed a culture of learning from mistakes that has led to significant improvements in safety.

Continuous Improvement: The pursuit of continuous improvement means that even when things are going well, there is always room for improvement. This means constantly looking for ways to do things better, even when you are succeeding.

Don't Blame Individuals: Blaming individuals for mistakes often leads to a culture of fear and secrecy, which hinders learning and innovation. Instead, focus on the system and processes that led to the mistake and look for ways to improve them.

Be Patient: Learning from mistakes takes time and effort. It requires patience and persistence to overcome the natural human tendency to avoid failure and to create a culture of learning and improvement.

Don't Give Up: Failure is a natural part of the learning process, and the only way to truly fail is to give up and stop trying. By persevering and learning from mistakes, you can achieve great things.

Summary

"Black Box Thinking" by Matthew Syed explores why some people and organizations are able to learn from their mistakes and improve, while others are not. The author draws on examples from a variety of fields, including aviation, healthcare, and sport, to illustrate how a culture of learning from failure can lead to significant improvements.

Syed argues that a key factor in this process is adopting a growth mindset, which involves being open to failure and seeing it as an opportunity to learn and improve. He also emphasizes the importance of reflection and continuous improvement, as well as creating an environment that encourages openness and transparency.

The book highlights the importance of innovation and experimentation, and how taking risks and learning from failures can lead to breakthroughs and significant improvements. The author also stresses the need to focus on the system and processes that lead to mistakes, rather than blaming individuals.

Overall, "Black Box Thinking" offers a compelling argument for the importance of embracing failure and learning from mistakes in order to achieve long-term success and improvement.

80. Thinking, Fast and Slow by Daniel Kahneman

Quotes

"We are confident when the story we tell ourselves comes easily to mind, with no contradiction and no competing scenario."

"The confidence that individuals have in their beliefs depends mostly on the quality of the story they can tell about what they see, even if they see little."

"The idea that the future is unpredictable is undermined every day by the ease with which the past is explained."

"Nothing in life is as important as you think it is when you are thinking about it."

"What you see is not all there is."

"The world in our heads is not a precise replica of reality; our expectations about the frequency of events are distorted by the prevalence and emotional intensity of the messages to which we are exposed."

"The illusion that we understand the past fosters overconfidence in our ability to predict the future."

"We often confuse what we know with what we think we know."

"Our comforting conviction that the world makes sense rests on a secure foundation: our almost unlimited ability to ignore our ignorance."

"It is easier to construct a coherent story when you know little, when there are fewer pieces to fit into the puzzle."

Lessons

"Thinking, Fast and Slow" is a groundbreaking book by Daniel Kahneman, a Nobel Prize-winning psychologist, which outlines the two systems that drive the way we think. Here are some of the key lessons from the book:

There are two modes of thinking: System 1 and System 2. System 1 operates automatically and quickly, while System 2 is more deliberate and requires conscious effort.

System 1 thinking is prone to errors and biases, which can lead to poor decision-making. System 2 thinking is more reliable, but it can also be prone to errors if it's overtaxed or if it's not used properly.

Our minds are influenced by a wide range of cognitive biases, including anchoring, framing, and confirmation bias. These biases can lead us to make flawed judgments and decisions.

The availability heuristic is a cognitive bias that causes us to overestimate the importance of information that's easily accessible to us, while ignoring information that's more difficult to obtain.

The sunk cost fallacy is a cognitive bias that causes us to persist with a course of action even when it's not in our best interests, simply because we've already invested time, money, or effort into it.

The planning fallacy is a cognitive bias that causes us to underestimate the time, resources, and effort required to complete a task or project.

The halo effect is a cognitive bias that causes us to form an overall positive or negative impression of a person, brand, or product based on one or a few specific traits or experiences.

Emotions play a critical role in decision-making, and our emotional state can influence our perceptions and judgments.

We tend to focus on the most salient features of a situation or problem, and ignore or downplay less salient factors. This can lead us to overlook important information and make poor decisions.

Cognitive biases and heuristics can be overcome with conscious effort and self-awareness. By slowing down and engaging in more deliberate, systematic thinking, we can reduce the impact of these biases on our decision-making.

Overall, "Thinking, Fast and Slow" provides a fascinating insight into the workings of our minds and the factors that influence our decisions. It's an essential read for anyone interested in psychology, decision-making, or human behavior.

Summary

Daniel Kahneman is that human decision-making is not always rational, objective, or accurate. The book presents evidence from cognitive psychology and behavioral economics that our brains use two distinct systems of thinking: "System 1" (fast, intuitive, and emotional) and "System 2" (slow, deliberate, and logical).

Kahneman argues that System 1 thinking often dominates our decision-making, leading to errors and biases. He describes numerous cognitive biases, such as the availability heuristic (judging the likelihood of an event based on how easily it comes to mind), the confirmation bias (seeking out information that confirms our beliefs), and the framing effect (being influenced by the way information is presented).

Another key lesson from the book is that we can learn to overcome some of these biases by being aware of them and engaging in deliberate, effortful System 2 thinking. By slowing down, questioning our assumptions, seeking out diverse perspectives, and using analytical tools, we can make better decisions and avoid common errors.

Overall, the book provides a fascinating and thought-provoking exploration of the human mind and how it shapes our perceptions, judgments, and actions. The lessons it offers can help individuals and organizations improve their decision-making processes and avoid costly mistakes.

CHAPTER 17

Networking and Relationships

81. Never Eat Alone: And Other Secrets to Success, One Relationship at a Time by Keith Ferrazzi and Tahl Raz

Quotes

"Success in any field, but especially in business, is about working with people, not against them."

"The real currency of any economy is not money, but trust."

"The more you give to others, the more you'll get in return. That's the way the world works."

"Your network is your net worth."

"The most successful people in the world are not the smartest, the most talented, or even the richest. They are the ones who surround themselves with a network of trusted friends and advisors."

"The best way to build a relationship is to find a common interest or goal and work together to achieve it."

"Networking is not about collecting contacts, it's about building relationships."

"The key to successful networking is to focus on what you can give, not what you can get."

"The best way to get to know someone is to ask questions and listen to their answers."

"Never eat alone. Food is one of the most powerful relationship-building tools we have."

Lessons

Building relationships is essential to success: The authors emphasize that building strong relationships is essential to achieving success in business and life. They argue that success is not only about what you know, but also who you know and how you interact with them.

Be proactive and reach out to others: The book stresses the importance of being proactive and reaching out to others. The authors encourage readers to take the initiative and make the effort to build relationships with people who can help them achieve their goals.

Build a diverse network: The authors emphasize the importance of building a diverse network of contacts from different industries, backgrounds, and levels of seniority. They argue that having a diverse network can open up new opportunities and perspectives.

Help others without expecting anything in return: The book emphasizes the importance of giving to others without expecting anything in return. The authors argue that helping others is a powerful way to build strong relationships and gain the trust of others.

Be authentic and genuine: The authors stress the importance of being authentic and genuine in building relationships. They argue that people can quickly detect insincerity, so it's important to be yourself and build relationships based on mutual respect and trust.

Attend events and conferences: The authors suggest attending events and conferences as a way to meet new people and build relationships. They argue that these types of events offer opportunities to meet people who share similar interests and goals.

Stay in touch with your network: The authors stress the importance of staying in touch with your network and nurturing your relationships over time. They suggest reaching out to your contacts regularly and keeping them updated on your progress.

Overall, "Never Eat Alone" is a powerful reminder of the importance of building relationships and networking as a crucial element of achieving success in business and life. The book provides practical strategies and advice for building and nurturing relationships, and emphasizes the importance of giving to others without expecting anything in return.

Summary

"Never Eat Alone" by Keith Ferrazzi and Tahl Raz is a book that emphasizes the importance of building strong relationships and networking as a crucial element of achieving success in business and life. The authors argue that success is not only about what you know but also who you know and how you interact with them.

The book provides practical strategies and advice for building and nurturing relationships, including the importance of being proactive and reaching out to others, building a diverse network, helping others without expecting anything in return, being authentic and genuine, attending events and conferences, and staying in touch with your network.

The authors emphasize that the most successful people in the world are those who surround themselves with a network of trusted friends and advisors. They argue that networking is not about collecting contacts but about building relationships based on mutual respect and trust. The book also emphasizes the importance of giving back to your community and building relationships based on shared values and interests.

Overall, "Never Eat Alone" is a powerful reminder of the importance of building relationships and networking as a crucial element of achieving success in business and life. The book provides practical strategies and advice for building and nurturing relationships, and emphasizes the importance of giving to others without expecting anything in return.

82. The Art of Possibility: Transforming Professional and Personal Life by Rosamund Stone Zander and Benjamin Zander

Quotes

"It's all invented anyway, so we might as well invent a story or a framework of meaning that enhances our quality of life and the life of those around us."

"We can choose to focus on the downward spiral of fear and resistance, or we can focus on the upward spiral of growth and possibility."

"The practice of giving an A allows people to experience themselves and others in a way that is both affirming and energizing."

"The way we see the world creates the world we see."

"When we become immersed in a reality of possibility, we see opportunities for action everywhere."

"We are not just a bundle of conditioned reflexes, but rather we have the capacity to create, to be innovative, to be resourceful, and to be whole."

"Leadership involves creating a climate where people's gifts are recognized and valued, and where everyone feels they are part of a common enterprise."

"The secret of transformation is to focus not on the problems but on the possibilities - on what we want to create instead of what we want to avoid."

"If you want to give an A, you have to be willing to enter into a partnership with the people you are giving it to."

"In the world of possibility, we are not separate from one another, and we are not separate from the world."

Lessons

The Art of Possibility is a book that offers powerful insights and practical advice for transforming our professional and personal lives. Here are some of the key lessons that can be learned from the book:

Embrace the Mindset of Possibility: The authors suggest that we can transform our lives by adopting a mindset of possibility. Instead of focusing on what's wrong or what we can't do, we can choose to focus on what's possible and what we can create.

Give an A: The authors argue that we can empower ourselves and others by giving an A - by treating everyone as if they are already doing their best. This means focusing on the positive and giving people the benefit of the doubt, which can help to create a culture of excellence and collaboration.

Be a Contribution: The authors suggest that we can transform our professional and personal lives by focusing on how we can contribute to others. This means looking for opportunities to help and serve, rather than just focusing on our own needs and desires.

Focus on the Whole System: The authors argue that we can't achieve real transformation by focusing on individual parts of a system. Instead, we need to look at the whole system and see how everything is interconnected. This means looking for solutions that benefit everyone, not just ourselves.

Change Your Story: The authors suggest that we can transform our lives by changing the stories we tell ourselves. Instead of seeing ourselves as victims or as limited by our circumstances, we can choose to see ourselves as capable of creating new possibilities and making a difference.

Lead from Possibility: The authors argue that effective leadership involves creating a culture of possibility. This means recognizing and valuing the gifts of others, and creating a sense of shared purpose and vision.

Overall, The Art of Possibility is a powerful and inspiring book that offers a new way of looking at the world and our place in it. By adopting a mindset of possibility and focusing on our ability to create positive change, we can transform our lives and the lives of those around us.

Summary

The Art of Possibility is a book that offers a new perspective on how we can transform our professional and personal lives. The authors, Rosamund Stone Zander and Benjamin Zander, argue that we can create a better world by adopting a mindset of possibility and focusing on our ability to create positive change. They offer practical advice and powerful insights on how we can achieve this, including giving an A, being a contribution, focusing on the whole system, changing our story, and leading from possibility.

The book is divided into twelve chapters, each of which explores a different aspect of the authors' approach to transformation. They draw on their own experiences as leaders, coaches, and educators to illustrate their points, and use a range of stories and examples to demonstrate the power of possibility thinking. Throughout the book, the authors emphasize the importance of recognizing and valuing the gifts of others, and creating a culture of collaboration and shared purpose.

Overall, The Art of Possibility is a compelling and inspiring book that challenges readers to think differently about their lives and their potential. It offers practical strategies for achieving transformation and creating a better world, and encourages readers to see themselves as agents of positive change.

83. Give and Take: Why Helping Others Drives Our Success by Adam Grant

Quotes

"Givers succeed not because they are doormats, but because they consistently add value to others - and in doing so, they are valued in return."

"The more I help out, the more successful I become. But I measure success in what it has done for the people around me. That is the real accolade."

"The greatest untapped source of motivation, he argues, is a sense of service to others; focusing on the contribution of our work to other people's lives has the potential to make us more productive than thinking about helping ourselves."

"People who give more, receive more in return. In this way, giving can fuel success, and vice versa."

"If we create networks with the sole intention of getting something, we won't succeed. We can't pursue the benefits of networks; the benefits ensue from investments in meaningful activities and relationships."

"Givers are the most successful people in life because of their focus on building supportive networks, collaborating with others and using their talents to help others."

"Success is not the key to happiness. Happiness is the key to success. If you love what you are doing, you will be successful."

"The most successful people are those who are able to harness their intrinsic motivation and use it to drive their careers and personal lives."

"Givers are motivated to help others not only because of a sense of duty or obligation, but because it brings them joy and fulfillment."

"When takers win, there's usually someone else who loses. Research shows that people tend to envy successful takers and look for ways to knock them down a notch. In contrast, when givers win, people are rooting for them and supporting them, rather than gunning for them."

Lessons

Being a giver can lead to success: Contrary to popular belief, it is not just the takers who succeed in life. Givers who focus on adding value to others can also achieve great success and be highly valued in return.

Collaboration and networking are essential: Building supportive networks and collaborating with others can lead to success, as it creates opportunities for growth and learning.

Helping others brings joy and fulfillment: Givers are motivated to help others not just out of obligation or duty, but because it brings them joy and fulfillment.

Focusing on the contribution of our work to other people's lives can increase motivation and productivity: When we focus on the impact of our work on others, it can help to increase our motivation and productivity, leading to greater success.

Giving can fuel success: Giving can lead to success and vice versa, as people tend to support and root for successful givers, rather than trying to bring them down.

Being generous doesn't mean being a pushover: Givers can be successful without being doormats. By setting boundaries and balancing their own needs with the needs of others, givers can find a healthy balance that leads to success.

Success is not the key to happiness, happiness is the key to success: Finding joy and fulfillment in what we do can lead to greater success, rather than just focusing on external measures of success.

We should focus on investing in meaningful activities and relationships: Rather than pursuing the benefits of networking, we should focus on investing in meaningful activities and relationships that can lead to success and happiness.

Givers tend to be more satisfied with their lives: Research shows that givers tend to be more satisfied with their lives than takers or matchers, as helping others brings them joy and fulfillment.

Summary

"Give and Take: Why Helping Others Drives Our Success" by Adam Grant is a book that explores the concept of giving and taking in personal and professional relationships. The book argues that givers, those who focus on adding value to others, can be just as successful as takers, who focus on taking from others.

The book presents research and real-life examples to support the idea that giving leads to success in many areas of life, including business, education, and personal relationships. It also examines how givers can avoid being taken advantage of and maintain a healthy balance between their own needs and the needs of others.

The book provides practical advice on how to be a successful giver, such as setting boundaries, finding ways to add value to others, and building supportive networks. It also discusses the benefits of collaboration and networking, as well as the importance of finding joy and fulfillment in our work and relationships.

Overall, "Give and Take" offers a new perspective on success, emphasizing the importance of helping others and building meaningful relationships. It is a thought-provoking read that challenges the traditional view of success as a zero-sum game and encourages readers to adopt a giving mindset to achieve success and happiness.

84. How to Talk to Anyone: 92 Little Tricks for Big Success in Relationships by Leil Lowndes

Quotes

"The single most important key to success in life is the ability to communicate effectively with others."

"To be interesting, be interested."

"Make the other person feel important – and do it sincerely."

"The biggest compliment you can give someone is your undivided attention."

"When you speak, use simple language and short sentences."

"Speak with conviction, even if you're not sure you're right."

"Don't criticize, condemn, or complain."

"Remember that a person's name is to that person the sweetest and most important sound in any language."

"Mirror the other person's body language to create rapport."

"Find common ground and build on it."

"Use humor to break the ice and ease tension."

"Listen with your eyes as well as your ears."

"Ask open-ended questions to encourage the other person to talk."

"Never underestimate the power of a sincere compliment."

"Make the other person feel good about themselves, and they'll want to be around you more."

Lessons

The importance of communication: Effective communication is key to success in both personal and professional relationships.

The power of listening: To build strong relationships, you need to be a good listener. By giving someone your full attention, you show that you value and respect them.

The importance of making people feel important: People respond positively when they feel valued and appreciated. Make an effort to make the people you interact with feel important and special.

The value of nonverbal communication: Nonverbal cues such as body language and tone of voice can be just as important as the words you use. Be aware of your nonverbal cues and learn to read those of others.

The importance of finding common ground: People are more likely to connect with others who share common interests or experiences. Look for common ground with the people you interact with.

The power of humor: Humor can be a great way to break the ice and ease tension in social situations.

The importance of being genuine: People can sense when someone is being fake or insincere. Be yourself and be honest in your interactions with others.

The value of positive reinforcement: People respond well to positive feedback and compliments. Learn to give sincere compliments and positive reinforcement.

The importance of confidence: Confidence is attractive and can help you make a good impression. Learn to speak with conviction and project confidence in your interactions with others.

The value of empathy: Being able to see things from another person's perspective can help you connect with them and build stronger relationships. Practice empathy in your interactions with others.

Summary

"How to Talk to Anyone: 92 Little Tricks for Big Success in Relationships" by Leil Lowndes is a self-help book that offers tips and tricks on how to improve your communication skills and build stronger relationships with others.

The book provides 92 different techniques that readers can use to become more confident, engaging, and effective communicators. Some of the key lessons from the book include the importance of being a good listener, making people feel important, finding common ground, using humor, and being genuine.

Lowndes emphasizes the importance of nonverbal communication and teaches readers how to use body language, tone of voice, and other nonverbal cues to enhance their communication skills. She also offers advice on how to give compliments, offer positive feedback, and practice empathy in order to build stronger connections with others.

Overall, "How to Talk to Anyone" is a practical and accessible guide that can help readers improve their communication skills, build better relationships, and achieve greater success in both their personal and professional lives.

85. The Charisma Myth: How Anyone Can Master the Art and Science of Personal Magnetism by Olivia Fox Cabane

Quotes

"Charisma is not a gift, it's a learnable skill. It can be acquired by anyone."

"Presence is the ability to be fully engaged in the moment, free from distraction or judgment, and aware of yourself and your surroundings."

"Power is the ability to project confidence and authority, to take charge of a situation, and to influence others through your words and actions."

"Warmth is the ability to connect with others on a deep level, to understand their needs and perspectives, and to communicate in a way that builds trust and rapport."

"The way you carry yourself physically can affect your mood, your energy level, and your ability to connect with others."

"Charismatic people are often very skilled at making others feel important and valued."

"Listening is one of the most powerful communication tools at your disposal."

"The more you can relate to someone else's perspective, the easier it is to connect with them on an emotional level."

"Authenticity is crucial to building trust and credibility with others."

"The best way to build confidence is to take action and step outside of your comfort zone."

Lessons

Charisma is a learnable skill: Charisma is not a natural talent that some people possess and others do not. It can be learned and developed by anyone who is willing to put in the effort.

Presence is essential: Being fully present in the moment, free from distractions and judgment, is essential to developing charisma. By practicing mindfulness and other techniques, you can learn to cultivate a strong sense of presence.

Power comes from body language and vocal tone: Nonverbal cues such as body language and vocal tone can have a powerful impact on how others perceive you. By learning to project confidence and authority through these cues, you can enhance your charisma and influence.

Warmth is critical for building relationships: Connecting with others on an emotional level is essential for building trust and rapport. By demonstrating empathy, active listening, and positive communication, you can develop your warmth and build stronger relationships.

Authenticity is key: Being true to yourself and your values is essential for building trust and credibility with others. By being honest and transparent, you can enhance your authenticity and improve your ability to connect with others.

Confidence comes from taking action: The best way to build confidence is to take action and step outside of your comfort zone. By challenging yourself and taking risks, you can develop your confidence and enhance your charisma.

Overall, "The Charisma Myth" provides a practical and science-backed guide to developing and enhancing your personal magnetism. By applying the lessons learned from the book, you can improve your social skills, enhance your leadership abilities, and achieve greater success in your personal and professional life.

Summary

"The Charisma Myth: How Anyone Can Master the Art and Science of Personal Magnetism" is a book written by Olivia Fox Cabane that offers practical advice and techniques for developing and enhancing one's charisma.

The book is divided into three sections, each focusing on a different aspect of charisma: presence, power, and warmth.

The first section, "Presence," emphasizes the importance of being fully present in the moment and developing a strong sense of self-awareness. Cabane offers several techniques for achieving this, such as mindfulness meditation and visualization exercises.

The second section, "Power," explores the ways in which individuals can project confidence and authority through body language, vocal tone, and other nonverbal cues. Cabane also offers advice on how to handle difficult situations and conversations with poise and grace.

The third section, "Warmth," focuses on the importance of building strong relationships with others through empathy, listening skills, and positive communication. Cabane offers tips on how to connect with others on a deeper level and foster a sense of trust and rapport.

Overall, "The Charisma Myth" is a practical guide for anyone looking to enhance their personal magnetism and develop their leadership and communication skills. Cabane's techniques are backed by scientific research and real-world examples, making this book a valuable resource for anyone seeking to improve their social skills and influence.

CHAPTER 18

Mindfulness and Meditation

86. 10% Happier: How I Tamed the Voice in My Head, Reduced Stress Without Losing My Edge, and Found Self-Help That Actually Works--A True Story by Dan Harris

Quotes

"Meditation suffers from a towering PR problem... people hear the word 'meditation' and immediately picture a monotone monk chanting in a temple. This is both unfortunate and misguided. Meditation is not about 'getting calm'; it's about learning to pay attention."

"The only way to be truly satisfied is to do what you believe is great work. And the only way to do great work is to love what you do."

"The problem with being a good sport is that you are still a loser."

"The voice in our head is constantly judging, comparing, labeling, and narrating."

"Happiness, in my experience, is a skill, not a trait. It requires effort, attention, and practice. Some days are better than others."

"Meditation is not a panacea, but there's certainly a lot of evidence that it may do some good for some people. What I can say for sure is that it's radically changed my life."

"I'm not saying we should all stop trying to improve ourselves. I'm just saying that perfection is not the goal. We're not supposed to be perfect. We're supposed to be complete - which is something very different."

"The key to success, I think, is to be grateful, and to be grateful you need to stop worrying about being constantly upgraded."

"The point is that instead of becoming paralyzed by rejection and failure, you can use them as further opportunities for growth."

"The ego, however, is relentless. It is always seeking a stronger foothold, always looking for the next way to assert itself, always on the lookout for a better deal."

Lessons

Meditation can be a powerful tool for reducing stress, improving focus, and increasing happiness.

The voice in our head is often critical and judgmental, and we can learn to tame it through mindfulness and meditation.

Success doesn't necessarily lead to happiness, and the pursuit of perfection can be self-defeating.

Accepting our imperfections and focusing on personal growth can lead to greater happiness and success.

Learning to be present in the moment and pay attention to our thoughts and feelings can help us better manage stress and anxiety.

Mindfulness and meditation can help us become more resilient in the face of challenges and setbacks.

It's important to approach self-help and personal development with a healthy dose of skepticism and to seek out evidence-based practices.

Practicing gratitude and focusing on the positives in our lives can help us cultivate greater happiness and well-being.

It's possible to be both ambitious and mindful, and incorporating mindfulness practices into our daily routines can help us achieve our goals.

Cultivating compassion and kindness toward ourselves and others can lead to greater happiness and fulfillment.

Summary

"10% Happier" is a memoir by journalist Dan Harris about his journey to find greater happiness and inner peace. After experiencing a panic attack on live television, Harris began exploring various self-help and mindfulness practices, ultimately finding solace in meditation. Through his own experiences and conversations with experts in the field, Harris offers insights into the benefits of mindfulness and meditation for reducing stress, improving focus, and increasing happiness. He also reflects on the pitfalls of perfectionism and the importance of self-compassion. The book is a candid and relatable exploration of the challenges of modern life and the potential for personal growth and transformation through mindfulness practices.

87. The Miracle of Mindfulness: An Introduction to the Practice of Meditation by Thich Nhat Hanh

Quotes

"The present moment is filled with joy and happiness. If you are attentive, you will see it."

"Feelings come and go like clouds in a windy sky. Conscious breathing is my anchor."

"The most precious gift we can offer anyone is our attention."

"The true miracle lies in our eagerness to allow, appreciate, and honor the uniqueness, and freedom of each sentient being to sing the song of their heart."

"Drink your tea slowly and reverently, as if it is the axis on which the world earth revolves - slowly, evenly, without rushing toward the future."

"The mind can go in a thousand directions, but on this beautiful path, I walk in peace. With each step, the wind blows. With each step, a flower blooms."

"Breathing in, I calm my body. Breathing out, I smile. Dwelling in the present moment, I know this is a wonderful moment."

"If we are peaceful, if we are happy, we can smile, and everyone in our family, our entire society, will benefit from our peace."

"Smile, breathe, and go slowly."

"To be beautiful means to be yourself. You don't need to be accepted by others. You need to accept yourself."

Lessons

Mindfulness is a powerful tool for finding peace and happiness in the present moment.

Mindfulness is about being fully present and engaged in the moment, rather than being distracted by thoughts about the past or future.

Mindfulness can be practiced in every aspect of our daily lives, from eating and drinking to walking and working.

Mindfulness can help us break free from our habitual patterns of thinking and behaving, and can help us become more compassionate and understanding toward others.

Mindfulness is not just a practice of sitting still and meditating, but can also be practiced through everyday activities like washing the dishes or brushing our teeth.

Mindfulness requires effort and practice, but it can bring great rewards in terms of increased peace, happiness, and well-being.

Mindfulness can help us cultivate a greater sense of gratitude and appreciation for the beauty of life and the world around us.

Mindfulness can also help us develop greater compassion and understanding for ourselves and others, which can improve our relationships and enhance our sense of connection to the world.

Summary

The Miracle of Mindfulness by Thich Nhat Hanh is a book about the practice of mindfulness and meditation. The book teaches readers how to cultivate mindfulness in every aspect of their lives, from eating and drinking to working and walking. Nhat Hanh explains that mindfulness is about being fully present and engaged in the moment, rather than being distracted by thoughts about the past or future. He emphasizes that mindfulness can help us break free from our habitual patterns of thinking and behaving, and can help us become more compassionate and understanding toward others. The book provides practical guidance and exercises for practicing mindfulness, including breathing techniques and meditation practices. Throughout the book, Nhat Hanh emphasizes the importance of cultivating a sense of gratitude, appreciation, and compassion in our daily lives. Overall, The Miracle of Mindfulness is a valuable guide to the practice of mindfulness and meditation, offering readers practical tools for finding peace and happiness in the present moment.

88. The Power of Now: A Guide to Spiritual Enlightenment by Eckhart Tolle

Quotes

"The power for creating a better future is contained in the present moment: You create a good future by creating a good present."

"Realize deeply that the present moment is all you have. Make the NOW the primary focus of your life."

"The mind is a superb instrument if used rightly. Used wrongly, however, it becomes very destructive."

"Most humans are never fully present in the now, because unconsciously they believe that the next moment must be more important than this one. But then you miss your whole life, which is never not now."

"Whatever the present moment contains, accept it as if you had chosen it. Always work with it, not against it."

"You are not separate from the whole. You are one with the sun, the earth, the air. You don't have a life. You are life."

"All negativity is caused by an accumulation of psychological time and denial of the present. Unease, anxiety, tension, stress, worry - all forms of fear - are caused by too much future, and not enough presence."

"The moment you realize you are not present, you are present. Whenever you are able to observe your mind, you are no longer trapped in it."

"The more you live in the present moment, the more the fear of death disappears."

"To be free of time is to be free of the psychological need of past for your identity and future for your fulfillment."

Lessons

The power of the present moment: The book emphasizes that the only thing that exists is the present moment, and that true happiness and enlightenment can only be found by living fully in the present and letting go of the past and future.

The nature of the ego: Tolle explores the nature of the ego and how it creates suffering by constantly seeking to validate its own existence and comparing itself to others. He suggests that we can learn to transcend the ego and access our true nature by becoming more present.

The importance of awareness: The book emphasizes the importance of becoming more aware of our thoughts, feelings, and behaviors, and learning to observe them without judgment or attachment.

The illusion of time: Tolle argues that time is an illusion created by the mind, and that true enlightenment involves transcending the limitations of time and accessing the timeless nature of the universe.

The power of acceptance: Tolle suggests that we can find greater peace and fulfillment by learning to accept the present moment exactly as it is, rather than constantly seeking to change it.

The interconnectedness of all things: The book emphasizes the interconnectedness of all things and suggests that true happiness and enlightenment can only be found by recognizing and embracing our connection to the larger universe.

The importance of meditation: Tolle suggests that meditation can be a powerful tool for accessing the present moment and learning to transcend the limitations of the ego.

Overall, "The Power of Now" teaches us to live more fully in the present moment, let go of our attachment to the past and future, and connect more deeply with our true nature and the larger universe.

Summary

"The Power of Now: A Guide to Spiritual Enlightenment" by Eckhart Tolle is a book that teaches readers how to achieve spiritual enlightenment by living fully in the present moment. The book emphasizes that the only thing that exists is the present moment, and that true happiness and enlightenment can only be found by letting go of the past and future and embracing the present moment. Tolle explores the nature of the ego, the illusion of time, and the interconnectedness of all things, and suggests that meditation can be a powerful tool for accessing the present moment and transcending the limitations of the ego. Overall, "The Power of Now" offers a transformative perspective on the nature of reality and the human experience, and provides practical tools for achieving greater peace, happiness, and spiritual fulfillment.

89. Mindfulness in Plain English by Bhante Henepola Gunaratana

Quotes

"The essence of meditation practice is to bring the mind home to the present moment."

"The problem is not with the object of desire, but with the craving for that object. It's the craving that causes our problems."

"Meditation is not evasion; it is a serene encounter with reality."

"Don't cling to your thoughts or your perceptions of reality. They are ephemeral and ultimately unsatisfying."

"The mind that is not yet calm enough to concentrate will naturally wander. Be patient with it."

"The past is gone, the future is not yet here, and if we do not go back to ourselves in the present moment, we cannot be in touch with life."

"The mind can become a faithful servant or a terrible master. The choice is yours."

"The breath is the anchor that we use to stabilize our attention in the present moment."

"You can't change the past, but you can ruin a perfectly good present by worrying about the future."

"It is not the object of meditation that counts, but the act of meditating itself."

Lessons

The importance of being present: One of the main lessons of the book is that we should strive to be fully present in the moment, rather than dwelling on the past or worrying about the future. By being mindful and aware of our thoughts and sensations in the present, we can reduce stress and anxiety and enjoy life more fully.

The value of meditation: Bhante Gunaratana emphasizes the benefits of meditation as a way to cultivate mindfulness and concentration. He explains various techniques for meditation and encourages readers to make a regular practice of it.

The role of acceptance and non-judgment: The book emphasizes the importance of accepting our thoughts and emotions as they arise, without judging them as good or bad. This helps us to avoid getting caught up in negative thinking patterns and to develop a more balanced and compassionate approach to life.

The power of letting go: Another lesson from the book is the importance of letting go of attachment and clinging to things. This can be difficult, but it is an important step towards inner peace and happiness.

The need for sustained effort: Finally, Bhante Gunaratana emphasizes that mindfulness and meditation require sustained effort and practice. It is not a quick fix, but a lifelong journey towards greater awareness and inner peace.

Summary

"Mindfulness in Plain English" by Bhante Henepola Gunaratana is a guide to meditation and mindfulness practice. The book emphasizes the importance of being fully present in the moment and cultivating mindfulness as a way to reduce stress, anxiety, and suffering. Bhante Gunaratana explains various meditation techniques, such as breathing and walking meditation, and encourages readers to make a regular practice of them. He also emphasizes the role of acceptance and non-judgment, and the power of letting go of attachment and clinging. The book emphasizes that mindfulness and meditation require sustained effort and practice, and that they can bring greater awareness and inner peace to our lives. Overall, "Mindfulness in Plain English" is a practical and accessible guide to mindfulness and meditation for anyone seeking to reduce stress and cultivate greater awareness and happiness in their life.

90. Wherever You Go, There You Are: Mindfulness Meditation in Everyday Life by Jon Kabat-Zinn

Quotes

"Wherever you go, there you are."

"Mindfulness is about being fully awake in our lives. It is about perceiving the exquisite vividness of each moment."

"The little things? The little moments? They aren't little."

"You can't stop the waves, but you can learn to surf."

"The present moment is the only time that any of us have to be alive - to know anything - to perceive - to learn - to act - to change - to heal."

"Meditation is not about feeling a certain way. It's about feeling the way you feel."

"Mindfulness is simply being aware of what is happening right now without wishing it were different; enjoying the pleasant without holding on when it changes (which it will); being with the unpleasant without fearing it will always be this way (which it won't)."

"To pay attention, this is our endless and proper work."

"As long as you are breathing, there is more right with you than there is wrong, no matter how ill or how hopeless you may feel."

"Mindfulness practice means that we commit fully in each moment to be present; inviting ourselves to interface with this moment in full awareness, with the intention to embody as best we can an orientation of calmness, mindfulness, and equanimity right here and right now."

Lessons

The importance of being present: The book teaches the importance of being present in the moment, rather than dwelling on the past or worrying about the future. Mindfulness practice can help individuals develop an awareness of the present moment, which can lead to greater peace and happiness.

The benefits of meditation: Kabat-Zinn describes the benefits of meditation, including stress reduction, improved concentration, and greater self-awareness. He also provides practical guidance on how to establish a daily meditation practice.

The power of acceptance: Mindfulness practice involves accepting things as they are, rather than trying to change or control them. Kabat-Zinn encourages readers to cultivate a non-judgmental awareness of their thoughts and feelings, which can lead to greater peace and happiness.

The role of compassion: The book emphasizes the importance of self-compassion and compassion for others. Mindfulness practice can help individuals develop greater empathy and understanding, leading to stronger relationships and a greater sense of well-being.

The value of simplicity: Kabat-Zinn encourages readers to simplify their lives and focus on what truly matters. Mindfulness practice can help individuals let go of distractions and appreciate the beauty of the present moment.

The interconnectedness of all things: The book encourages readers to recognize the interconnectedness of all things and to develop a sense of gratitude for the world around them. Mindfulness practice can help individuals develop a greater appreciation for the natural world and a deeper understanding of their place in it.

Overall, the book teaches the importance of mindfulness practice as a means to live a more fulfilling and meaningful life.

Summary

"Wherever You Go, There You Are: Mindfulness Meditation in Everyday Life" is a book by Jon Kabat-Zinn that explores the practice of mindfulness in everyday life. The book teaches the importance of being present in the moment, cultivating self-awareness, and developing a non-judgmental awareness of thoughts and feelings.

Kabat-Zinn emphasizes the benefits of meditation, including stress reduction, improved concentration, and greater self-awareness. He provides practical guidance on how to establish a daily meditation practice and encourages readers to simplify their lives and focus on what truly matters.

The book also teaches the importance of compassion for oneself and others, and encourages readers to recognize the interconnectedness of all things and develop a sense of gratitude for the world around them.

Overall, "Wherever You Go, There You Are" is a guide to mindfulness practice that can help readers live a more fulfilling and meaningful life..

CHAPTER 19
Sales and Marketing

91. The Challenger Sale: Taking Control of the Customer Conversation by Brent Adamson and Matthew Dixon

Quotes

"The Challenger Sale is a new approach to selling that is rooted in the belief that our customers' needs have changed fundamentally over the past decade or so - and that our approach to selling must change along with them."

"Challengers are characterized by a deep understanding of their customers' businesses and a desire to teach their customers something new and valuable about how their businesses can improve."

"The Challenger Sale is about taking control of the customer conversation, challenging the status quo, and ultimately, leading the customer to a better solution."

"The most successful sales reps today are those who can offer insights and advice that customers haven't heard before, and who can use those insights to challenge the customer's thinking."

"The Challenger Sale is not about being confrontational or aggressive. Rather, it's about being confident and assertive in a way that encourages the customer to think differently about their business."

"The best Challengers are those who can create a sense of constructive tension in the customer conversation - a tension that motivates the customer to change and take action."

"The Challenger Sale is not a one-size-fits-all approach. Rather, it requires reps to be highly adaptable, constantly learning, and willing to experiment with new approaches."

"The key to success as a Challenger is to focus on the customer's business outcomes, rather than just their own sales targets."

"Challengers are successful because they are able to establish credibility and build trust with their customers by demonstrating deep knowledge of their customers' businesses and showing a genuine interest in helping them succeed."

"The Challenger Sale is not just about selling - it's about building long-term, mutually beneficial relationships with customers."

Lessons

Customers today are looking for sales reps who can provide them with valuable insights and challenge their thinking, rather than just pushing a product or service.

To be successful in sales, reps need to have a deep understanding of their customers' businesses, and be able to offer new ideas and advice that the customer hasn't heard before.

Successful sales reps are those who can create a sense of constructive tension in the customer conversation - challenging the customer's thinking in a way that motivates them to change and take action.

The key to success as a Challenger is to focus on the customer's business outcomes, rather than just their own sales targets.

The Challenger Sale is not a one-size-fits-all approach - it requires reps to be highly adaptable, constantly learning, and willing to experiment with new approaches.

Building long-term, mutually beneficial relationships with customers is essential to success in sales.

The best Challengers are those who can establish credibility and build trust with their customers by demonstrating deep knowledge of their customers' businesses and showing a genuine interest in helping them succeed.

The Challenger Sale is not about being confrontational or aggressive - it's about being confident and assertive in a way that encourages the customer to think differently about their business.

Sales reps who are successful in The Challenger Sale are those who are willing to invest time and effort in researching and understanding their customers' businesses, and in developing new insights and ideas to share with them.

The Challenger Sale is a new approach to selling that requires a shift in mindset and behavior for sales reps, but the rewards in terms of sales success and customer satisfaction can be significant.

Summary

"The Challenger Sale" by Brent Adamson and Matthew Dixon is a book that presents a new approach to selling. The authors argue that customers today are looking for sales reps who can provide them with valuable insights and challenge their thinking, rather than just pushing a product or service. Successful sales reps, or "Challengers," are those who have a deep understanding of their customers' businesses, and can offer new ideas and advice that the customer hasn't heard before. They create a sense of constructive tension in the customer conversation, challenging the customer's thinking in a way that motivates them to change and take action.

The key to success as a Challenger is to focus on the customer's business outcomes, rather than just their own sales targets. Building long-term, mutually beneficial relationships with customers is essential to success in sales. The best Challengers are those who can establish credibility and build trust with their customers by demonstrating deep knowledge of their customers' businesses and showing a genuine interest in helping them succeed.

The Challenger Sale is not a one-size-fits-all approach - it requires reps to be highly adaptable, constantly learning, and willing to experiment with new approaches. Sales reps who are successful in The Challenger Sale are those who are willing to invest time and effort in researching and understanding their customers' businesses, and in developing new insights and ideas to share with them.

Overall, "The Challenger Sale" is a practical guide for sales reps and sales leaders who want to take control of the customer conversation, challenge the status quo, and ultimately, lead the customer to a better solution. The book provides concrete strategies and tactics for implementing the Challenger approach, and offers insights into the behaviors and skills that are essential for success in sales today.

92. To Sell Is Human: The Surprising Truth About Moving Others by Daniel H. Pink

Quotes

"Like it or not, we're all in sales now."

"The ability to move others to exchange what they have for what we have is crucial to our survival and our happiness."

"Sales has changed. Today, it's less about selling products and services than it is about serving others."

"To sell well is to convince someone else to part with resources - not to deprive that person, but to leave him better off in the end."

"Attunement is the ability to bring one's actions and outlook into harmony with other people and with the context you're in."

"Clarity is about making sense of murky situations by developing a clear sense of what's going on and what's important."

"Buoyancy is the quality that allows us to stay afloat amid the ocean of rejection we face every day in sales."

"To sell is human because selling requires us to persuade and influence others to take action."

"The purpose of selling is not to move products, but to serve others by solving problems and meeting needs."

"The most effective sellers are those who are able to tell compelling stories that resonate with their audience."

Lessons

Everyone is in sales: The ability to influence, persuade, and convince others to take action is a critical skill that applies to many aspects of our lives.

Attunement is important: To be effective at selling, we need to understand and empathize with the needs and perspectives of our audience.

Clarity is crucial: We need to be able to communicate clearly and succinctly to ensure that our message is understood.

Buoyancy is essential: To be successful in sales, we need to be able to handle rejection and maintain a positive attitude.

We need to serve, not sell: Effective sales is about solving problems and meeting the needs of our customers, rather than just pushing products or services on them.

Storytelling is powerful: By telling compelling stories that resonate with our audience, we can connect with them on an emotional level and move them to action.

Honesty and integrity are critical: Building trust with our customers is essential for long-term success in sales.

Selling is a learning process: We need to be open to feedback, continually learning, and adapting our approach to meet the needs of our audience.

We need to focus on creating value: By creating value for our customers, we can build strong, long-lasting relationships that benefit everyone involved.

Sales is a human endeavor: To be successful in sales, we need to approach it as a human endeavor that is rooted in relationships, communication, and understanding.

Summary

"To Sell Is Human: The Surprising Truth About Moving Others" by Daniel H. Pink explores the modern landscape of sales, arguing that selling is no longer just the domain of salespeople, but something that we all do in our personal and professional lives. Through research and real-world examples, Pink outlines a new approach to selling that emphasizes empathy, problem-solving, and service. He identifies three key qualities that are essential for effective selling: attunement, or the ability to understand and connect with the needs and perspectives of our audience; buoyancy, or the ability to handle rejection and maintain a positive attitude; and clarity, or the ability to communicate clearly and succinctly. He also highlights the power of storytelling as a way to connect with others on an emotional level and move them to action. Throughout the book, Pink emphasizes the importance of honesty, integrity, and building strong relationships with customers. Overall, "To Sell Is Human" offers a fresh perspective on the art of selling, challenging traditional notions of what it means to sell and highlighting the importance of empathy, service, and creativity in today's sales landscape.

93. "Never Split the Difference: Negotiating As If Your Life Depended On It" by Chris Voss

Quotes

"The most dangerous negotiation is the one you don't know you're in."

"Negotiation is not an act of battle; it's a process of discovery. The goal is to uncover as much information as possible."

"The words people use are like fingerprints; they reveal a lot about who they are and what they want."

"The person who has the most information has the greatest leverage in a negotiation."

"The key to great negotiation is being able to articulate the other person's position better than they can."

"The most powerful tool in a negotiation is the ability to walk away from the table without a deal."

"The person who can control their emotions and thoughts during a negotiation is the one who will ultimately come out on top."

"Negotiation is not about being right, it's about getting the best possible outcome for yourself."

"Don't be afraid to ask for what you want in a negotiation. The worst they can say is no."

"The most successful negotiators are the ones who can create win-win situations, where both parties walk away feeling like they got a good deal."

Lessons

Use empathy and active listening: Empathy is a powerful tool in negotiation, as it helps to build trust and rapport with the other party. Active listening is also crucial, as it allows you to understand the other party's perspective and needs.

Focus on the other party's emotions: People's emotions play a significant role in negotiations, so it's essential to understand and acknowledge them. Addressing emotions can help to diffuse tense situations and create a more productive negotiation environment.

Don't be afraid to ask questions: Asking the right questions can provide valuable information and help to clarify the other party's position. It can also help to uncover underlying motivations and interests.

Use anchoring: Anchoring is the process of setting an initial offer or price, which can influence the other party's perception of the negotiation. Setting an initial anchor that is favorable to you can help to improve your negotiation position.

Practice tactical empathy: Tactical empathy involves using empathy strategically to influence the other party's behavior and decisions. It can be used to build trust, gain information, and shape the negotiation in your favor.

Create a feeling of safety: Creating a sense of safety and trust can help to foster a more productive negotiation environment. This can be achieved by listening actively, acknowledging emotions, and showing empathy.

Be prepared: Preparation is key to successful negotiations. This includes researching the other party, understanding their needs and motivations, and having a clear idea of your own goals and priorities.

Don't split the difference: Splitting the difference can result in a suboptimal outcome for both parties. Instead, focus on creating value and finding creative solutions that benefit everyone.

Be willing to walk away: Walking away from a negotiation can be a powerful tool. It shows that you are willing to prioritize your own interests and can put pressure on the other party to make concessions.

Aim for win-win outcomes: Successful negotiations often result in win-win outcomes, where both parties feel satisfied with the outcome. This requires finding creative solutions and identifying areas where both parties can benefit.

Summary

"Never Split the Difference" by Chris Voss is a book on negotiation that draws on the author's experience as an FBI hostage negotiator. The book provides practical tips and strategies for negotiating effectively in a variety of situations, including business deals, personal relationships, and high-pressure situations.

Voss emphasizes the importance of active listening, empathy, and understanding the other party's emotions and motivations. He suggests using tactical empathy to influence the other party's behavior and create a feeling of safety and trust. He also emphasizes the importance of preparation and setting clear goals and priorities.

The book highlights the importance of creating win-win outcomes that benefit both parties, rather than simply splitting the difference. Voss provides strategies for creating value and finding creative solutions that can benefit everyone.

The book also covers specific negotiation techniques, such as anchoring, labeling, and mirroring. It emphasizes the importance of being willing to walk away from a negotiation and not settling for suboptimal outcomes.

Overall, "Never Split the Difference" is a comprehensive guide to negotiation that provides practical tips and strategies for negotiating effectively in a variety of situations.

94. Made to Stick: Why Some Ideas Survive and Others Die by Chip Heath and Dan Heath

Quotes

"A successful idea is one that is made to stick, is understood, remembered, and influences thought and behavior."

"The key to making an idea stick is to make it simple, unexpected, concrete, credible, emotional, and tell a story."

"Curiosity is the gateway to learning and the foundation for creating a lasting impression."

"We need to break our ideas down to their core and focus on the most essential elements."

"If you say three things, you say nothing."

"A powerful message doesn't just inform, it stimulates the imagination and engages the audience."

"The more we know about a topic, the harder it is for us to communicate it to others. We need to focus on the most important aspects and simplify the message."

"Telling a story is one of the most effective ways to make an idea stick, as it engages the emotions and captures the imagination."

"In order for an idea to stick, it must have an emotional component that resonates with the audience."

"To make an idea sticky, we need to tap into the core values and beliefs of our audience."

Lessons

Simplicity is crucial: Ideas that are easy to understand are more likely to stick than those that are complex and convoluted.

Unexpectedness is powerful: People remember things that surprise them or go against their expectations.

Concreteness helps ideas stick: Abstract ideas are harder to grasp and remember than concrete ones.

Credibility is key: People are more likely to believe and remember ideas that come from a trustworthy source.

Emotion plays a role: Ideas that evoke strong emotions are more likely to stick in people's minds.

Stories are effective: Stories are a powerful tool for conveying ideas and making them memorable.

Focus on the essential: It's important to distill ideas down to their core and focus on the most important aspects.

Communicate with your audience in mind: To make ideas stick, you need to understand your audience and communicate in a way that resonates with them.

Repetition helps: Repeating key points or ideas can help them stick in people's minds.

Test your ideas: To know whether an idea is likely to stick, you need to test it with real people and see how they respond.

Summary

"Made to Stick: Why Some Ideas Survive and Others Die" by Chip Heath and Dan Heath is a book that explores why some ideas are more memorable and impactful than others. The authors identify six key principles that make ideas "stick": simplicity, unexpectedness, concreteness, credibility, emotions, and stories. They provide numerous examples of successful and unsuccessful ideas, and analyze them through the lens of these principles. The book also emphasizes the importance of testing ideas and understanding your audience in order to make an idea truly sticky. Overall, "Made to Stick" offers practical advice for anyone looking to communicate ideas effectively and make them more memorable and impactful.

95. Crossing the Chasm: Marketing and Selling High-Tech Products to Mainstream Customers by Geoffrey A. Moore

Quotes

"Without a sound marketing strategy, a technology breakthrough can be just another pretty invention languishing in the laboratory."

"The chasm is the yawning gap between the early adopters and the early majority."

"The key to crossing the chasm is to focus on a single niche market and dominate it."

"The key to winning the early majority is not to prove that your product is better, but to prove that it is not going to cause them any problems."

"Visionaries want to be the first to try something new. They are willing to take risks to achieve their goals. Pragmatists want to be the second to try something new. They want to learn from the experiences of the visionaries."

"The biggest mistake companies make is trying to cross the chasm with a product that is not yet ready for prime time."

"The key to successful marketing in the technology adoption life cycle is to align your strategy with the dominant buying criteria of each group."

"Marketing is not about providing information, it is about eliciting a response."

"The four most dangerous words in business are 'We've always done it that way.'"

"To create a successful high-tech product, you need to identify a significant customer problem, develop a breakthrough solution, and bring it to market before the competition."

Lessons

Identify your target market: To successfully sell a high-tech product, you need to identify your target market and focus on dominating it. This means understanding the needs and preferences of your target customers and creating a product that meets those needs.

Understand the technology adoption lifecycle: The technology adoption lifecycle consists of five stages - innovators, early adopters, early majority, late majority, and laggards. Each stage has different buying criteria and requires a different marketing approach.

Focus on the early majority: The early majority is the largest group of customers and the key to achieving mainstream success. To win over this group, you need to focus on solving their problems and addressing their concerns.

Create a compelling value proposition: Your product needs to offer a clear and compelling value proposition that differentiates it from the competition. This means highlighting the benefits that your product offers and how it solves a specific problem.

Develop a sound marketing strategy: A sound marketing strategy is essential for success in the high-tech industry. This means understanding your target market, developing a clear value proposition, and identifying the right channels to reach your customers.

Build a strong team: Success in the high-tech industry requires a strong team that is committed to achieving your goals. This means hiring the right people, fostering a culture of innovation, and providing the necessary resources and support.

Be adaptable: The high-tech industry is constantly evolving, and you need to be adaptable to succeed. This means being open to feedback, continuously improving your product, and being willing to pivot your strategy when necessary.

Take calculated risks: To succeed in the high-tech industry, you need to take calculated risks. This means investing in research and development, exploring new markets, and being willing to try new things. However, it is important to balance risk with caution and avoid taking unnecessary risks that could harm your business.

Summary

"Crossing the Chasm: Marketing and Selling High-Tech Products to Mainstream Customers" by Geoffrey A. Moore is a book that focuses on the challenges of marketing and selling high-tech products to mainstream customers. The book provides a framework for understanding the technology adoption lifecycle and outlines a strategy for crossing the chasm between early adopters and the early majority.

Moore argues that early adopters are different from the early majority and require a different marketing approach. He suggests that companies should focus on dominating a single niche market before expanding to other markets. The book provides case studies and examples of companies that successfully crossed the chasm and achieved mainstream success.

The book also emphasizes the importance of building a strong team, developing a sound marketing strategy, and taking calculated risks. Moore highlights the need for a compelling value proposition, a clear understanding of the target market, and the right channels to reach customers.

Overall, "Crossing the Chasm" is a valuable resource for anyone involved in marketing and selling high-tech products. The book provides practical advice and actionable strategies for achieving mainstream success in the high-tech industry.

CHAPTER 20
Leadership and Management
96. Good to Great: Why Some Companies Make the Leap and Others Don't by Jim Collins

Quotes

"Good is the enemy of great."

"When [what you are deeply passionate about, what you can be best in the world at and what drives your economic engine] come together, not only does your work move toward greatness, but so does your life."

"Level 5 leaders channel their ego needs away from themselves and into the larger goal of building a great company. It's not that Level 5 leaders have no ego or self-interest. Indeed, they are incredibly ambitious -- but their ambition is first and foremost for the institution, not themselves."

"Greatness is not a function of circumstance. Greatness, it turns out, is largely a matter of conscious choice, and discipline."

"The good-to-great companies did not say, "Okay, folks, let's get passionate about what we do." Sensibly, they went the other way entirely; We should only do those things that we can get passionate about."

"The moment you feel the need to tightly manage someone, you've made a hiring mistake. The best people don't need to be managed. Guided, taught, led—yes. But not tightly managed."

"In a world of constant change, the fundamentals are more important than ever."

"It is not the technology that determines what is possible or impossible. It is our use of technology that determines what is possible or impossible."

"The purpose of bureaucracy is to compensate for incompetence and lack of discipline."

"If you have more than three priorities, then you don't have any."

Lessons

Start with the right people: According to the book, one of the most important factors in moving a company from good to great is having the right people on the bus. That means hiring talented and motivated individuals who are a good fit for your organization.

Focus on your core business: Great companies tend to focus on what they do best, rather than chasing after new opportunities or diversifying too much. This requires discipline and a willingness to say no to opportunities that don't align with your core business.

Develop a culture of discipline: The book argues that great companies have a culture of discipline, in which employees are focused on doing the right things, rather than just doing things. This requires clear goals, metrics, and accountability.

Embrace technology wisely: The book argues that technology can be a powerful enabler of growth and efficiency, but it should be used wisely. Great companies use technology strategically to enhance their core business, rather than chasing after the latest fads.

Be humble and open to change: The book argues that great companies are led by humble, Level 5 leaders who are willing to admit mistakes and learn from them. These leaders are also open to change and willing to embrace new ideas and perspectives.

Stay focused on the long-term: The book argues that great companies have a long-term perspective and are willing to invest in the future, even if it means sacrificing short-term profits. This requires a willingness to delay gratification and stay the course through tough times.

Overall, the key lesson from Good to Great is that achieving greatness requires a combination of strategic focus, disciplined execution, and a culture of excellence.

Summary

Good to Great is a business book written by Jim Collins that aims to answer the question of what separates great companies from merely good ones. Collins and his team of researchers analyzed companies that made the leap from good to great over a 15-year period and compared them to similar companies that did not make the transition. The book outlines the common characteristics and practices of the great companies, and offers insights into how other companies can follow their lead.

Some of the key findings in the book include the importance of having the right people on the team, focusing on your core business, developing a culture of discipline, embracing technology wisely, being humble and open to change, and staying focused on the long-term. The book argues that great companies are led by Level 5 leaders who are able to channel their ego needs into building a great company, rather than seeking personal glory.

Overall, Good to Great is a well-researched and practical guide for companies looking to achieve greatness. It emphasizes the importance of disciplined execution, strategic focus, and a culture of excellence, and offers actionable advice for companies looking to improve their performance and make the leap from good to great.

97. The 7 Habits of Highly Effective People: Powerful Lessons in Personal Change by Stephen R. Covey

Quotes

"Begin with the end in mind."

"The key is not to prioritize what's on your schedule, but to schedule your priorities."

"Most people do not listen with the intent to understand; they listen with the intent to reply."

"The way we see the problem is the problem."

"Seek first to understand, then to be understood."

"The main thing is to keep the main thing the main thing."

"Interdependent people combine their own efforts with the efforts of others to achieve their greatest success."

"To change ourselves effectively, we first had to change our perceptions."

"We are not human beings on a spiritual journey. We are spiritual beings on a human journey."

"Synergy is the highest activity of life; it creates new untapped alternatives; it values and exploits the mental, emotional, and psychological differences between people."

Lessons

Be proactive: Take control of your life and focus on what you can control, rather than reacting to external factors.

Begin with the end in mind: Define your long-term goals and work towards them in a proactive way.

Put first things first: Prioritize your tasks and activities based on importance, not urgency.

Think win-win: Seek mutually beneficial solutions in your relationships and interactions with others.

Seek first to understand, then to be understood: Listen actively to others and seek to understand their perspective before sharing your own.

Synergize: Work collaboratively with others to achieve more than you could individually.

Sharpen the saw: Take care of yourself physically, mentally, emotionally, and spiritually to maintain your overall well-being.

Overall, the book teaches that effectiveness is not just about getting things done efficiently, but also about cultivating strong relationships, living with purpose, and maintaining balance in all areas of life. By adopting these seven habits, individuals can become more effective in both their personal and professional lives.

Summary

"The 7 Habits of Highly Effective People" is a self-help book by Stephen R. Covey that presents a framework for personal growth and development. The book is based on the idea that success in life is not just about achieving goals, but about living a balanced and fulfilling life. Covey identifies seven habits that he believes are key to achieving this balance and developing effectiveness in all areas of life. These habits are:

1. Be proactive
2. Begin with the end in mind
3. Put first things first
4. Think win-win
5. Seek first to understand, then to be understood
6. Synergize
7. Sharpen the saw

Through anecdotes, personal stories, and practical exercises, Covey explains how these habits can be applied to improve personal and professional relationships, increase productivity, and achieve greater overall success. The book has become a classic in the self-help genre, with millions of copies sold worldwide and a lasting impact on popular culture. Its message of personal responsibility and holistic growth has inspired countless individuals to take control of their lives and pursue their goals with purpose and intention.

98. Start with Why: How Great Leaders Inspire Everyone to Take Action by Simon Sinek

Quotes

"People don't buy what you do, they buy why you do it."

"There are only two ways to influence human behavior: you can manipulate it or you can inspire it."

"The goal is not to do business with everyone who needs what you have. The goal is to do business with people who believe what you believe."

"Working hard for something we don't care about is called stress; working hard for something we love is called passion."

"Great leaders are those who trust their gut. They are those who understand the art before the science. They win hearts before minds."

"If you hire people just because they can do a job, they'll work for your money. But if you hire people who believe what you believe, they'll work for you with blood and sweat and tears."

"People don't follow what you do, they follow why you do it."

"The more organizations and people who learn to start with WHY, the more people there will be who wake up being fulfilled by the work they do."

"When people are financially invested, they want a return. When people are emotionally invested, they want to contribute."

"Authenticity is when you say and do the things you actually believe."

Lessons

Start with Why: Sinek argues that great leaders and organizations start with WHY they do what they do, not with WHAT they do or HOW they do it. By starting with WHY, they inspire others to follow them and create a sense of purpose that drives their success.

The Golden Circle: Sinek introduces the Golden Circle, a framework for understanding how great leaders and organizations communicate. The Golden Circle consists of three concentric circles: WHY (the purpose or belief that inspires them), HOW (the way they bring their purpose to life), and WHAT (the tangible products or services they offer).

The Power of Belief: Sinek emphasizes the importance of belief in inspiring action. When people believe in a cause or a leader, they are more likely to be committed, loyal, and passionate. Belief creates a sense of purpose and meaning that drives action.

Emotions Drive Action: Sinek argues that people make decisions based on emotions, not logic. Great leaders understand this and appeal to people's emotions by telling stories and creating experiences that inspire them.

The Importance of Culture: Sinek emphasizes the importance of culture in driving behavior and creating success. Leaders who create a strong culture based on shared values and beliefs are more likely to inspire their employees, attract loyal customers, and achieve long-term success.

The Role of Authenticity: Sinek argues that authenticity is crucial for inspiring trust and loyalty. Leaders who are genuine, honest, and transparent are more likely to be trusted by their followers and create lasting relationships.

The Power of Innovation: Sinek encourages leaders to embrace innovation and take risks. By experimenting and trying new things, leaders can create new opportunities and stay ahead of the competition.

Overall, "Start with Why" teaches us that great leaders and organizations are driven by purpose, inspire belief, appeal to emotions, create strong cultures, and embrace innovation. By understanding these principles, we can all become better leaders and inspire others to take action.

Summary

"Start with Why" by Simon Sinek is a book about leadership and how great leaders inspire action. Sinek argues that the most successful leaders and organizations start with WHY they do what they do, rather than focusing solely on WHAT they do or HOW they do it. By starting with WHY, leaders can inspire others to follow them and create a sense of purpose that drives their success.

Sinek introduces the Golden Circle, a framework for understanding how great leaders and organizations communicate. The Golden Circle consists of three concentric circles: WHY (the purpose or belief that inspires them), HOW (the way they bring their purpose to life), and WHAT (the tangible products or services they offer). Sinek emphasizes the importance of belief in inspiring action, and argues that people make decisions based on emotions, not logic.

Sinek also emphasizes the importance of culture in driving behavior and creating success. Leaders who create a strong culture based on shared values and beliefs are more likely to inspire their employees, attract loyal customers, and achieve long-term success. Authenticity is crucial for inspiring trust and loyalty, and leaders who are genuine, honest, and transparent are more likely to be trusted by their followers and create lasting relationships.

Overall, "Start with Why" teaches us that great leaders and organizations are driven by purpose, inspire belief, appeal to emotions, create strong cultures, and embrace innovation. By understanding these principles, we can all become better leaders and inspire others to take action.

99. The Lean Startup: How Today's Entrepreneurs Use Continuous Innovation to Create Radically Successful Businesses by Eric Ries

Quotes

"The goal of a startup is to figure out the right thing to build – the thing customers want and will pay for – as quickly as possible."

"A startup is a human institution designed to create a new product or service under conditions of extreme uncertainty."

"The only way to win is to learn faster than anyone else."

"The most important thing a startup can do is focus on creating a minimum viable product (MVP) as quickly as possible."

"The key to the lean startup method is to quickly build a minimum viable product, test it with real customers, and use the feedback to guide further development."

"Innovation is a bottoms-up, decentralized, and unpredictable thing, but that doesn't mean it can't be managed."

"The lean startup method is not about cost-cutting or incremental improvement, it is about achieving fast, sustainable growth."

"The lean startup is not just about spending less money. It's about spending less time discovering the wrong thing."

"The most successful entrepreneurs are those who are willing to be wrong, learn from their mistakes, and keep moving forward."

"The lean startup is not a one-size-fits-all solution, but rather a framework for building and running a startup in a way that maximizes your chances of success."

Lessons

Start with a Minimum Viable Product (MVP): The lean startup methodology emphasizes the importance of quickly developing a minimum viable product (MVP) that can be tested with real customers. This helps entrepreneurs learn what works and what doesn't before investing too much time and resources into a product that may not have a market.

Use data-driven decision making: The lean startup methodology is all about using data to drive decision making. Instead of relying on assumptions and intuition, entrepreneurs should gather feedback from customers and use that data to guide their product development.

Embrace uncertainty: Startups are by their nature uncertain, and the lean startup methodology emphasizes the importance of embracing that uncertainty. Entrepreneurs should be prepared to pivot and change direction if they learn that their assumptions are wrong or if the market changes.

Build a culture of experimentation: Experimentation is at the heart of the lean startup methodology. Entrepreneurs should encourage a culture of experimentation and be willing to take risks, learn from failures, and iterate quickly.

Continuously innovate: The lean startup methodology emphasizes the importance of continuous innovation. Successful entrepreneurs should always be looking for new ways to improve their product, find new markets, and stay ahead of the competition.

Focus on customer needs: The lean startup methodology emphasizes the importance of focusing on customer needs. Entrepreneurs should develop a deep understanding of their customers and their needs, and use that knowledge to guide their product development.

Iterate quickly: The lean startup methodology emphasizes the importance of iterating quickly. Entrepreneurs should be willing to release imperfect products and iterate quickly based on customer feedback.

Create a sustainable business model: The lean startup methodology emphasizes the importance of creating a sustainable business model. Entrepreneurs should focus on creating a product that customers are willing to pay for and that can generate sustainable revenue over the long term.

Summary

"The Lean Startup: How Today's Entrepreneurs Use Continuous Innovation to Create Radically Successful Businesses" by Eric Ries is a book that presents a new approach to entrepreneurship that emphasizes rapid experimentation and continuous innovation. The book argues that the traditional approach to building a startup is flawed, as it often leads to waste and failure. Instead, the author advocates for a lean startup methodology that involves developing a minimum viable product (MVP) quickly and testing it with real customers. The book also emphasizes the importance of data-driven decision making, embracing uncertainty, and continuously innovating. The author provides many real-life examples of successful startups that have used the lean startup methodology to achieve rapid growth and success. Overall, the book provides a practical and actionable guide for entrepreneurs looking to build successful businesses in today's rapidly changing marketplace.

100. Drive: The Surprising Truth About What Motivates Us by Daniel H. Pink

Quotes

"When it comes to motivation, there's a gap between what science knows and what business does."

"The problem with making an extrinsic reward the only destination that matters is that some people will choose the quickest route there, even if it means taking the low road."

"Human beings have an innate inner drive to be autonomous, self-determined, and connected to one another. And when that drive is liberated, people achieve more and live richer lives."

"The best use of money as a motivator is to pay people enough to take the issue of money off the table."

"If you want to build a ship, don't drum up people to collect wood and don't assign them tasks and work, but rather teach them to long for the endless immensity of the sea."

"Goals that people set for themselves and that are devoted to attaining mastery are usually healthy. But goals imposed by others – sales targets, quarterly returns, standardized test scores, and so on – can sometimes have dangerous side effects."

"The ultimate freedom for creative groups is the freedom to experiment with new ideas. Some skeptics insist that innovation is expensive. In the long run, innovation is cheap. Mediocrity is expensive – and autonomy can be the antidote."

"One source of frustration in the workplace is the frequent mismatch between what people must do and what people can do. When what they must do exceeds their capabilities, the result is anxiety. When what they must do falls short of their capabilities, the result is boredom. But when the match is just right, the results can be glorious."

"Money can extinguish intrinsic motivation, diminish performance, crush creativity, encourage unethical behavior, foster short-term thinking, and become addictive."

"Greatness and nearsightedness are incompatible. Meaningful achievement depends on lifting one's sights and pushing toward the horizon."

Lessons

Autonomy, mastery, and purpose are key drivers of motivation: People are motivated when they have the autonomy to choose what they do, the opportunity to become masters at it, and a sense of purpose that goes beyond mere profit.

Rewards and punishments are not effective motivators for complex tasks: Rewards and punishments work for simple, straightforward tasks, but they can actually hinder performance on complex tasks that require creativity and problem-solving.

Money is not the most important motivator: While money is important, it is not the only or even the most important motivator. In fact, excessive focus on money can actually demotivate people and lead to unethical behavior.

Intrinsic motivation is more powerful than extrinsic motivation: People are more motivated when they are driven by intrinsic factors such as curiosity, challenge, and the desire to learn, rather than extrinsic factors such as money or status.

Mastery is a lifelong pursuit: Mastery is not a destination, but a journey that requires continuous learning, experimentation, and improvement.

Autonomy requires trust: Giving people autonomy requires trust, and trust can only be built through transparency, communication, and respect.

Purpose is the ultimate motivator: People are most motivated when they feel that their work has a greater purpose beyond themselves, and when they feel that they are making a meaningful contribution to society.

Creativity thrives on autonomy and experimentation: Creativity is hindered by strict rules and micromanagement, but it thrives when people have the freedom to experiment and try new things.

A healthy workplace culture is essential for motivation: A workplace culture that values trust, transparency, respect, and open communication is essential for creating an environment that fosters motivation, creativity, and growth.

Motivation is a complex and multifaceted phenomenon: Motivation is influenced by a variety of factors, including individual differences, organizational culture, social norms, and external incentives. Understanding these factors is key to creating a motivated and engaged workforce.

Summary

"Drive: The Surprising Truth About What Motivates Us" by Daniel H. Pink is a book that explores the science of motivation and what truly drives us to do our best work. Pink argues that traditional motivators such as rewards and punishments are not effective for complex tasks that require creativity and problem-solving. Instead, he proposes that people are motivated by three key factors: autonomy, mastery, and purpose.

Autonomy refers to the desire to have control over our own lives and work. People are more motivated when they have the autonomy to choose what they do, how they do it, and when they do it. Mastery is the desire to improve and become better at something. People are motivated when they have the opportunity to develop their skills, experiment with new ideas, and learn from their mistakes. Purpose is the desire to contribute to something larger than ourselves. People are most motivated when they feel that their work has a greater purpose beyond themselves and that they are making a meaningful contribution to society.

Pink also discusses how traditional motivators such as money can actually demotivate people and lead to unethical behavior. Instead, he argues that intrinsic motivation, which comes from within, is more powerful and long-lasting than extrinsic motivation, which comes from external rewards such as money or status.

Throughout the book, Pink provides numerous examples of companies and organizations that have successfully implemented these principles to create a motivated and engaged workforce. He also provides practical tips and strategies for individuals and leaders to implement these principles in their own lives and workplaces.

Overall, "Drive" is a thought-provoking and insightful book that challenges traditional notions of motivation and provides a new framework for understanding what truly drives us to do our best work.

101. The One Minute Manager by Kenneth Blanchard and Spencer Johnson

Quotes

"People who feel good about themselves produce good results."

"The best minute I spend is the one I invest in people."

"Goals begin behaviors, consequences maintain behaviors."

"Feedback is the breakfast of champions."

"Catch people doing something right."

"Help people reach their full potential. Catch them doing something right."

"The key to successful leadership today is influence, not authority."

"When you make a mistake, admit it, correct it, and learn from it — immediately."

"People who feel good about themselves produce good results and people who produce good results feel good about themselves."

"Effective managers manage themselves and the people they work with so that both the organization and the people profit from their presence."

Lessons

Set One Minute Goals: Setting clear and concise goals is essential to achieving success. The One Minute Manager recommends setting one-minute goals that are specific, measurable, attainable, relevant, and time-bound.

Give One Minute Praisings: Catch people doing something right and give them immediate feedback. This creates a positive work environment and motivates people to continue doing good work.

Use One Minute Reprimands: When someone makes a mistake, address it immediately. The One Minute Manager recommends using a clear and concise reprimand that is focused on the behavior, not the person.

Empower People: Give people the freedom to take ownership of their work and make decisions. This leads to increased productivity and job satisfaction.

Practice Situational Leadership: The One Minute Manager recommends adapting your leadership style based on the situation and the needs of the individual. This means being flexible and able to provide the appropriate level of direction and support.

Focus on Results: The One Minute Manager emphasizes the importance of achieving results. It is not enough to simply go through the motions or look busy. Success comes from setting clear goals and taking action to achieve them.

Continuously Improve: The One Minute Manager encourages continuous improvement and learning. This means being open to feedback, seeking out new opportunities, and constantly looking for ways to improve performance.

Overall, "The One Minute Manager" teaches readers that effective management requires a focus on people, results, and continuous improvement. By setting clear goals, providing feedback, empowering people, and adapting your leadership style, you can create a positive work environment and achieve success.

Summary

"The One Minute Manager" by Kenneth Blanchard and Spencer Johnson is a concise guide to effective management that emphasizes simplicity, clarity, and focus on results. The book tells the story of a young man who is seeking to learn the secrets of effective management, and who is introduced to a manager who has achieved great success by following three simple principles: One Minute Goals, One Minute Praisings, and One Minute Reprimands.

One Minute Goals involve setting clear, specific, and measurable goals that are achievable and time-bound. The idea is to focus on what needs to be done, rather than how it will be done, and to ensure that everyone understands what is expected of them.

One Minute Praisings are a way to catch people doing things right and provide immediate positive feedback. The idea is to reinforce good behavior and create a positive work environment that motivates people to continue doing good work.

One Minute Reprimands are a way to address mistakes and provide immediate corrective feedback. The idea is to focus on the behavior, not the person, and to ensure that the person understands what they did wrong and how to correct it.

The book also emphasizes the importance of empowering people, practicing situational leadership, focusing on results, and continuously improving. By following these principles, the One Minute Manager achieves great success and creates a positive work environment that leads to increased productivity and job satisfaction.

Overall, "The One Minute Manager" is a simple yet powerful guide to effective management that emphasizes the importance of clear communication, feedback, and a focus on results. It is a must-read for anyone seeking to improve their management skills and create a positive work environment.

www.ingramcontent.com/pod-product-compliance
Lightning Source LLC
Chambersburg PA
CBHW070527220526
45467CB00003B/880